Workshops for the World

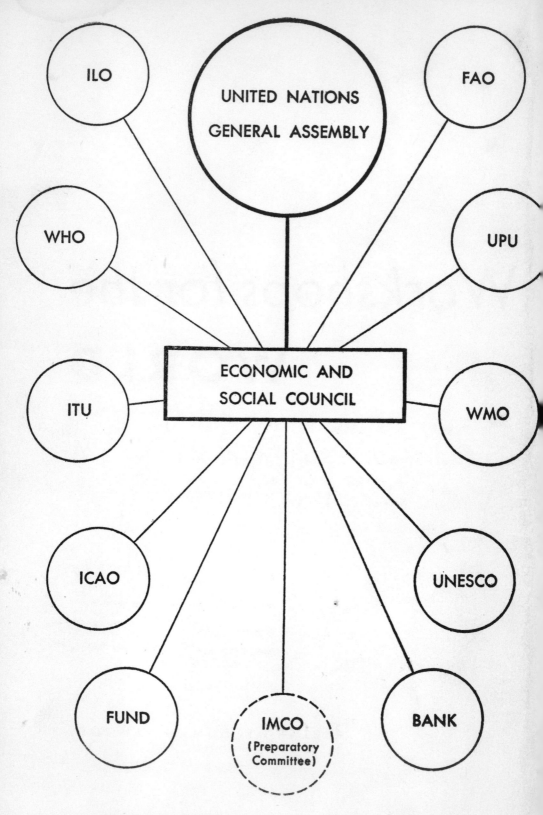

WORKSHOPS FOR THE WORLD

Workshops for the
WORLD

THE SPECIALIZED AGENCIES OF THE
UNITED NATIONS

By GRAHAM BECKEL

WITH AN INTRODUCTION BY
BENJAMIN A. COHEN
Asst. Secretary-General, United Nations

ABELARD-SCHUMAN, *NEW YORK*

COPYRIGHT, 1954, BY GRAHAM BECKEL

LIBRARY OF CONGRESS CATALOG CARD NUMBER: 53-11284

PRINTED AND BOUND IN THE UNITED STATES OF AMERICA

PUBLISHED SIMULTANEOUSLY IN CANADA

BY NELSON, FOSTER & SCOTT, LTD.

SECOND PRINTING

Dedicated to the personnel of the
International Civil Service

CONTENTS

LIST OF ILLUSTRATIONS

Frontispiece

CHAPTER 1: **FAO**

A balanced diet of fish and rice has been harvested.

Workmen are shown deepening an already existing pond in Haiti.

Dr. Lin supervises the transporting of carp and Tilapia fingerlings.

Tilapia fingerlings imported from Jamaica are placed in Haiti.

Sure that no danger threatens, a Tilapia releases the amazing number of young fish it has been guarding in its mouth.

Studying the comparative value of various artificial fish foods.

(Between pages 8 and 9)

FAO expert working with the fisheries officers of Bangkhen Fisheries Station on the selection of breeders.

Homeward bound after a hard day's work in the fish ponds.

Packing fish fingerlings for long-distance transport.

CHAPTER 2: **ICAO**

"Takeoff?"

A well coordinated system of communication is essential.

"Each member of the crew is a specialist in a particular field."

The U. S. Coast Guard Cutter *Spencer.*

As trans-Atlantic planes approach the *Spencer* the radar operator traces their courses on the twin screens.

Radioman aboard the *Spencer* talks with the pilot of a passing plane, relaying data for navigational use.

Internationally financed air navigation services of ICAO.

(Between pages 24 and 25)

Below deck, the course of an aircraft in distress over the open waters of the North Atlantic is charted by a crewman on a plotting board.

Trainees from various member nations of ICAO participate in a demonstration of the new ILA language for aviation.

The Council of the International Civil Aviation Organization.

CHAPTER 3: **WHO-UNICEF**

Mrs. Bille-Brahe keeps records of the health situation of mothers and children in a village in the WHO-UNICEF Malaria Control Team's area (Orissa, India).

An enlarged spleen marks this child as a Malaria victim.

Here is Nurse Bille-Brahe at the bedside of a plague victim.

(Between pages 40 and 41)

One of the 22 spraying squads working with the WHO-UNICEF team in the jungle villages of Orissa State (India).

Workers spray DDT for mosquito control in a village.

School children doing "Twig toothbrush" drill under the supervision of the WHO-UNICEF Malaria Control Team nurse and her local assistant.

School children in a Malnad village (Mysore State, India) go through "personal hygiene" drill.

CHAPTER 4: **UPU**

United Nations International Stamps.

For the convenience of philatelists and visitors to the United Nations Headquarters, stamps may be purchased for both philatelic and postage purposes.

(Between pages 56 and 57)

CHAPTER 5: **ILO**

Life is both hazardous and hard for the Rhine boatman.

Dutch Captain M. van Dam, owner of the Rhine boat *God mit Uns,* with his wife in their living quarters.

The wife of a seaman is shown hanging laundry on the deck.

The kitchen on board the *Richebourg.*

The grocery boat supplies goods to the wife of a Rhine boatman.

Captain G. Vermeeren, owner of the barge *Anna,* with his wife and three children.

Boarding school for children of the Rhine boatmen on a remodelled barge in Rotterdam harbor.

Crew of a German steam tug in their quarters.

The German Federal Republic is represented by government, worker, and employer delegates to the ILO Conference on Rhine Boatmen held at Geneva, Switzerland on 31 October 1949.

How the ILO works.

(Between pages 72 and 73)

CHAPTER 6: **ITU**

The overseas switchboard marked "Via Oakland" where calls originating in New York City for Djakarta are routed to the overseas operator in Oakland, California.

The overseas switchboard in Oakland, California where calls are handled between New York City and Djakarta.

An exterior view of the radio station at Dixon, California.

The overseas control terminal in Oakland, California where a technical operator maintains the radiotelephone circuit on calls to Djakarta.

Indonesian overseas operators receive calls from New York.

From Bandung the call goes by land wire to the central switchboard in Djakarta.

An operator in Djakarta uses the regular telephone system to reach the person for whom the call is intended.

View of the Palais Wilson in Geneva, Switzerland, Headquarters of the International Telecommunication Union.

(Between pages 88 and 89)

Any subscriber in the domestic telephone system can be connected with 80,900,000 telephones outside the continental limits of the United States.

(Page 92)

CHAPTER 7: **UNESCO**

This Tarascan woman is drawing water from a well in one of the villages near the Patzcuaro.

A typical Tarascan school child.

A typical class of Tarascan children in a village school near Patzcuaro. These schools are the cultural centers of the villages.

Students in the Reading Room and Library at the Fundamental Education Center Headquarters.

When the film strip and lecture notes are completed the film strip is tested in the villages.

The day after the showing students follow up the program by hanging posters on the same subject around the village.

(Between pages 92 and 93)

Miss Predard Garcia (Ecuadorian student) talking to a villager of Juaracuaro who has been persuaded to install a high hearth instead of cooking on the floor.

Inoculation of pigs against cholera.

A student shows a peasant from Opopeo, a mountain village near Patzcuaro, how to graft pear shoots on to a crab-apple tree.

Cottage and home industries can help to raise the economic level of the village. Here instruction is being given in straw-plaiting.

A modern harvester dragged by a bullock team.

CHAPTER 8: **Bank**

Groups of small farmers have joined together in cooperative associations to buy and use some of the agricultural machinery which was financed by the International Bank's $5 million loan to Colombia's Caja de Credito.

New areas are being added to the usable farm land of Colombia.

(Between pages 100 and 101)

A page from a reading primer produced by the students.

(Page 103)

A World Bank loan of $16.5 million is financing extensive highway repair and reconstruction.

Many of Colombia's roads twist and turn across mountainous terrain and part of the Bank's loan is financing the regrading of such stretches.

The La Insula generating plant is one of the three small hydroelectric stations which the Bank is helping finance in Colombia.

CHAPTER 9: **Fund**

The Articles of Agreement, International Monetary Fund, showing the signatures of representatives of Member governments.

Camille Gutt of Belgium and the Secretary-General of the United Nations sign the International Monetary Fund Protocol, 1948.

With this scroll the Government of Honduras expressed appreciation of the Fund's technical assistance in establishing the country's first central bank.

(Between pages 104 and 105)

The Headquarters of the International Monetary Fund.

President Aleman of Mexico addressing the Seventh Annual Meeting of the Fund's Board of Governors in Mexico City.

The Deputy Secretary of the Fund welcomes technical assistance trainees from the Philippines, India, Thailand, and Iran.

CHAPTER 10: **WMO**

A weather balloon is inflated and equipped with a radiosonde.

Analyzing weather bulletins for broadcast to shipping.

Analyzing surface and upper air charts.

(Between pages 120 and 121)

Weather reports are distributed to Weather Bureau offices by teletypewriter circuits.

Pilots being briefed before take-off as to weather conditions forecast over route.

Flag signalling in international code from a weather ship.

World Map of WMO Regions.

(Between pages 136 and 137)

CHAPTER 11: **IRO**

Mr. and Mrs. Alfreds Rolavs of Skookum Bay.

Mr. Rolavs contributes to the expansion of the Bishops' oyster and clam business.

Some of the refugees from IRO camps in Germany, Austria and Italy are shown boarding an IRO-chartered ship at Bremerhaven for the U.S.A.

Twelve-year-old Dace Epermanis (holding flowers) gets a special send-off at Bremerhaven, Germany, when records of the IRO disclosed that she was the 150,000th person to be admitted to the U.S.A. under its Displaced Persons law.

CHAPTER 12: **IMCO**

The officers of the United Nations Transport and Communications Commission: Mr. Willem L. De Vries (left) of the Netherlands, Chairman; and Sir H. Osborne Mance of the United Kingdom, Vice-Chairman.

The Government of Burma formally becomes a party to the convention of the Intergovernmental Maritime Consultative Organization. Mr. James Barrington (right), Representative of Burma, presents that country's acceptance to Mr. A. H. Feller, formerly Principal Director of the United Nations Legal Department.

France ratifies the IMCO Convention at United Nations Headquarters. Mr. Philippe de Seynes (left) presents the instrument of ratification to Mr. Ivan S. Kerno, Assistant Secretary-General in charge of the Legal Department.

(Between pages 152 and 153)

CHAPTER 13: **TEAMWORK**

United Nations—WHO-UNICEF technical assistance to the Philippines includes anti-TB campaigns.

Under the United Nations Technical Assistance Program FAO helps Ethiopia in the fight against rinderpest, the disease that at one time killed a million head of cattle yearly.

A UNESCO Technical Assistance Mission to Liberia trains skilled personnel needed for the country's developing economy. Dr. Henry C. McBay, of the United States, UNESCO teacher of chemistry, is shown explaining a problem to his class at Liberia College, Monrovia.

General view of a meeting of the Second Technical Assistance Conference held in Paris.

Partial view of a meeting of the Economic and Social Council. Representatives of the Specialized Agencies are seated to the right.

(Between pages 156 and 157)

CHAPTER 14: **U. S. in the Specialized Agencies**

Dr. Edward P. Warner (right), President of the Council of ICAO, is shown explaining an illustrated display of aerodromes and aerodrome equipment.

Mr. C. P. Vasudevan of India (left) is studying all aspects of long distance and trunk telephone systems with the American Telephone and Telegraph Company in New York City under the United Nations Technical Assistance Fellowship Program.

Mr. Montgomery Blair (1813-1883) who as Postmaster General of the United States was responsible for the first international postal conference in 1863.

Dr. F. W. Reichelderfer, President of the World Meteorological Organization (WMO) and Chief of the United States Weather Bureau.

Mr. Eugene R. Black.

Dr. Luther Evans.

(Between pages 164 and 165)

International Bank bonds are brought to the attention of American investors.

(Page 177)

INTRODUCTION

By Benjamin A. Cohen
Assistant Secretary-General, Public Information, UN

I AM VERY GLAD to welcome, on behalf of the United Nations Department of Public Information, the publication of "Workshops for the World." The author has used an intelligent way to describe the work of the United Nations Specialized Agencies. There are stories here which are interesting in themselves but which also have a particular importance as brought together in this book. The author performs a very useful service in bringing to public attention the international cooperation which goes forward daily towards the United Nations goal of a peaceful and better world for all people.

International cooperation in the economic and social fields is central to the concept of the United Nations and carries out one of the purposes of the organization stated in the Charter. It must be remembered that the United Nations Charter is not simply an instrument for the negotiation and settlement of political disputes. The Charter looks beyond political disputes to the basic causes of conflict in the world—poverty, hunger, disease, and the despair to which they lead. It charges the members of the United Nations to seek solutions to these problems and, in its words, to "promote higher standards of living, full employment and conditions of economic and social progress and development."

The Charter set out a program for achieving these ends and the framework in which they shall be pursued. First, the intergovernmental organizations already operating in the economic and social *fields were to be brought into relationship with the United Nations. These organizations with their special functions were hereafter to be called "Specialized Agencies." Second, new agencies were to be created wherever the United Nations might find them necessary to carry out its purposes of creating "conditions of stability and well being" in the world.*

These Specialized Agencies are independent organizations; each is established by separate intergovernmental agreement. Their own Charters specify their specific autonomous fields. But equally important is their interdependence, which flows from their common goal of fashioning a better world. Being thus united in purpose, these organizations had to be united in their working approach to the common goal. The United Nations Charter put the responsibility for this coordination upon the Economic and Social Council, which receives regular reports from the Specialized Agencies and through a process of consultation and recommendation develops a coordinated approach. The Council may also make recommendations for coordination to the General Assembly and to the members of the United Nations.

The administrative arm within the coordination framework is the Administrative Committee on Coordination, whose members are the Secretary-General of the United Nations and the executive heads of the Specialized Agencies. This Committee studies the program of work; it appraises and analyzes current needs and recommends priorities to the Economic and Social Council.

The interlocking of the United Nations and Agencies' program in the economic and social field is most clearly seen in the United Nations Expanded Program of Technical Assistance. This program was drawn up by the Secretary-General of the United Nations and the heads of eight Specialized Agencies in response to a request from the Economic and Social Council. It was subsequently approved by the General Assembly and is carried out by a Technical Assist-

ance Board consisting of all of the organizations which take part and a Technical Assistance Committee of all of the nations who are members of the Economic and Social Council.

The problems of hunger, disease, and poverty are intimately related. So, too, under the program of the United Nations and the Specialized Agencies many diverse skills have been related and joined together in a world-wide effort to solve these problems.

Benjamin A. Cohen

United Nations, New York
25 September 1953

AUTHOR'S PREFACE

On december 17, 1903, Orville and Wilbur Wright made their first flights at Kitty Hawk, North Carolina. In the fifty years that have gone by since then the idea of one world has become a geographic fact. Cities that were not even listed in the geography books our grandfathers used are now commonplace names to all of us. Most of these cities may be reached by simply picking up your telephone transmitter and asking for the long-distance operator. A person listening to a radio in Bombay, India, will hear the words of a speaker in New York before these same words are heard by the people sitting in the lecturer's audience.

However small our world has become, if we had the good fortune to make a trip around it by air we would discover that this world is made up of series of neighborhoods. As we looked down upon these neighborhoods we would discover that some of them are vast cities linked to the surrounding countryside by an intricate pattern of highways and railways, while others are merely clearings in the jungle reached by a simple foot trail cut through the underbrush. Between these two extremes would be other neighborhoods of varying sizes. No matter how many of these neighborhoods we might visit, we would find they each have one thing in common—the people in them are dependent upon one another. Each person takes a hand in creating goods or services that are used by his fellow men.

If we were to examine more carefully this exchange of goods

and services in our American society we would discover that many of our daily transactions depend upon the goods and services produced in other neighborhoods in other lands. Without these imports there would be no tea or coffee, no important metals to mix with our ore for making steel, no telephones, no radio or television tubes, and no automobiles. Some thirty-eight minerals vital to our industry are produced as goods and services by neighborhoods in other lands. Without these our life would be drab indeed.

In order to insure the sharing of resources between neighborhoods and nations, certain conditions are important. In the first place, there must be peace. We have banded together with other nations to create a world machine designed to solve the problem of peace. We call this machine the United Nations. Working together through this large organization we hope to harmonize the neighborhoods of the world so that goods and services, peoples and ideas, may flow freely among them.

But this is only part of the task. The problem of world peace is of a general nature. In addition there are the specific technical problems that directly concern the people who produce the goods, and the services that move goods and peoples from one national neighborhood to another. These problems deal with the health of the producers, with the food they eat and with the conditions under which they work. These problems deal with communication between the neighborhoods of the world, whether it be by mail, radio, or telephone. These problems involve the safe movement of peoples and goods by air, land, and sea. These problems may deal with the financing of new enterprises, the exchanges of currency, and the sharing of scientific and technical knowledge.

Problems like these require the services of experts in specialized fields of knowledge. Long before the establishment of the United Nations, many governments had already entered into agreements with governments of other nations to create agencies for the purpose of bringing together specialists in some of these fields. It was only natural that these organizations should be called *specialized agencies.*

When the Charter of the United Nations was drafted, provisions were made for bringing the established Agencies into working agreements with the United Nations. In addition to coordinating the work of existing agencies, procedures were established for creating new Agencies as well. A list of all the Agencies—both old and new—is given below, with the dates on which they formally came into being:

Universal Postal Union (UPU), 1875

International Labor Organization (ILO), 1919

International Telecommunication Union (ITU), 1932

Food and Agriculture Organization (FAO), 1945

International Bank for Reconstruction and Development (Bank), 1945

United Nations Educational, Scientific and Cultural Organization (UNESCO), 1946

International Monetary Fund (Fund), 1945

International Civil Aviation Organization (ICAO), 1947

World Health Organization (WHO), 1948

World Meteorological Organization (WMO), 1950

The International Refugee Organization (IRO) was established in 1948 and closed its operations in 1952. Two other Agencies have not been formally established: the Inter-Governmental Maritime Consultative Organization (IMCO) and the International Trade Organization (ITO).

The purpose of this book is to bring together in narrative form case studies of the Agencies at work. Because no two Agencies have identical membership, it would be impossible for the Agencies themselves to tell the collective story of their activities—although individual Agencies have done excellent jobs in their own publications of explaining their work. As a student, teacher, and member of numerous discussion groups the author has long felt the need of some one book that would present the significant contributions of the Agencies by telling how each accomplished a specific task, and at the same time would include basic reference material for each Agency. In addition, it seems important to know how Agencies come into being, how they team up with the United Nations, and the role that the United States plays in them.

The case study approach to the Specialized Agencies as described in this book had its origin in the author's classes in Modern World History at the Westfield (N. J.) Senior High School. We felt that the study of international cooperation and "know-how" should concern itself with situations we already knew something about. Telephones, radio, mail service, working conditions, planes, schools, doctors, food, banks, trade, and the weather were the stuff of our daily lives. As these matters were also the concern of the Specialized Agencies, a study of their operations seemed natural.

We began our study by asking ourselves a series of questions. What problems can we think of in getting a plane from the local airport to London? Of making a telephone call to Indonesia? Of helping the people of India rid themselves of malaria? These were typical of our self-questioning. In many instances our problems exceeded two hundred in number. We didn't find the answers to each problem then, and they won't all be found in this book. But we did make the exciting discovery that people can and do work together to solve these world neighborhood problems even though vast differences and distances separate them one from another. We discovered that in solving the problems of goods and services, man was waging peace.

In light of the foregoing I had planned to dedicate this book to those former students. They will be happy to learn that after meeting dozens of the people who are making the Agencies effective instruments for world peace I decided upon my dedication to the international civil service. Their day is here. Your contributions are yet to be!

So many people have cooperated in making this work possible that I have acknowledged their individual contributions at the end of the book.

GRAHAM BECKEL

Elizabeth, New Jersey
1 January 1954

FOREWORD

The conception, planning, and coordination of the Specialized Agencies is something new and significant in the search for a solution to the age-old problem of how neighborhoods may live more harmoniously together. Before examining the Agencies in more detail, it is well to keep in mind certain facts concerning them:

1. Each of the Specialized Agencies is separate from the United Nations and from all the others. Each Agency has its own charter, budget, governing body, and headquarters.

2. Each of the Specialized Agencies is, like the United Nations, a freely accepted organization of governments. Not all members of the United Nations are members of all the Specialized Agencies. Some members of individual Agencies are not members of the United Nations.

3. Each Agency has entered into a mutual working relationship with the United Nations that has been approved by the governing body of the Agency and by the General Assembly of the United Nations.

4. This relationship with the United Nations makes possible the coordination of the work of the Agencies through the planning of the Economic and Social Council of the United Nations.

5. *Generally speaking, the Agencies work out plans for action and suggest ways of carrying the action into effect. The responsibility for completing the action rests with the governments of member nations.*

6. *The activities of the Specialized Agencies influence the daily life pattern of individuals more directly than do most activities of the United Nations.*

1

FAO

PLANT AN ACRE OF FISH

Food and Agriculture Organization

WHO EVER HEARD of *planting* fish? To most Americans the title of this chapter reads like the beginning of a whopping big *fish* story. But to millions of people throughout the world the food produced by fish farming means the difference between an adequate diet and the ugly fact of hunger. And to millions more who have the opportunity to learn the science of fish farming, malnutrition from lack of the most important of all foodstuffs, the proteins, may be a thing of the past.

In some of the world's neighborhoods the art of fish farming is an age-old practice. The ancient Romans dug ditches that carried young salt-water fish into the low areas near the coast, where they were trapped and kept until large enough to be used for food. This same practice is followed today in certain parts of France and Italy. The raising of fresh-water fish dates back many centuries, particularly in the Far East. As early as the fifteenth century, historians report that the victorious tribes of Java forced their captives to the task of building huge fish ponds. If such a large-scale industry existed in Java in the 1400's, the art of fish culture must certainly have been known much earlier to Javanese farmers.

Other neighborhoods besides ancient Rome and Java had learned the rather simple facts that make fish farming possible. In the course of a year a body of water will produce a certain amount of fish food, such as plankton and algae. These and other plants can be used directly by fish that feed on water plants, and indirectly by those that feed on smaller fish. Rice fields lend themselves admirably to the cultivation of fish, since the thin layer of water over the paddy fields produces an abundant crop of fish food. When recently hatched fish (fry) are introduced into the field, an acre of such land is sufficient to produce from 45 to 135 pounds of fish in a three-month period. It doesn't come as a surprise, therefore, to learn that fish farming has been practiced for centuries in rice-growing countries like Indonesia, Japan and Vietnam, where, in some areas, 80 per cent of the rice fields are stocked with carp and other species of fish.

Unfortunately, this knowledge had not been independently discovered by all the peoples of the world. Nearly half of the world's population, mainly in tropical countries and particularly in the Caribbean area, suffer malnutrition from want of proteins. Yet hundreds of millions of these people live in neighborhoods where there are lakes, rivers, irrigation canals, and rice fields that could be made to yield a high production of fish. And fish are a rich source of protein! Help in spreading the "know-how" of fish farming to neighborhoods that need it is one of the services provided by the Food and Agriculture Organization.

One government making such use of FAO is the Republic of Haiti. The people of Haiti have long been faced with the fundamental problem of producing enough goods and services to provide for their steadily growing population. In 1948 the government of Haiti requested the United Nations to send a group of experts into the country to study the problem and to make suggestions for improving the life of the people. Professor Ernest F. Thompson of Yale University was the member of this mission assigned by the Food and Agriculture Organization to investigate the specific problem of food production.

In his report Professor Thompson noted, among many other things, that the fishing industry of Haiti is limited to small operations along the coast of the island. However, Haiti possesses a number of areas suitable for pond construction, and also rivers, irrigation canals, and lagoons rich in fish food. These could be utilized to raise large quantities of fish that would help solve the tragic problem of malnutrition and at the same time provide a prosperous new industry for the farmers. Professor Thompson recommended that the government of Haiti, working with the FAO, take the following action before deciding on a program of fish farming:

1. The services of a first-class fish-culture specialist familiar with practices in other countries should be employed to make an extended survey of the situation.

2. If after the survey the government of Haiti decided upon a program of fish farming, the services of the specialist should be retained for a number of years to guide the program.

3. At least two Haitians should be trained in the principles of fish culture to follow up the plans of the specialist.

The government of Haiti gave careful attention to Professor Thompson's report, and then requested FAO to assign a specialist for the purpose of carrying out the suggested survey. It was only natural that a person experienced in the fish-farming activities of the Far East should be chosen for this task. In June of 1950, Dr. S. Y. Lin was assigned to the fish-culture project in Haiti.

Dr. Lin was born on Hainan Island, China. Following his graduation from Yenching University in Peking he worked with the Kwangtung Fisheries Experiment Station in Canton, China. It was here that he began the studies in fisheries biology and fish culture that finally prepared him to take charge of a fisheries investigation project in the China Sea. When the Sino-Japanese War broke out in 1937, Dr. Lin went to the British colony of Hong Kong as a refugee. The

Hong Kong government made it possible for him to continue his studies, and when a Fisheries Research Station was established there in 1940 he became superintendent, a position he held until 1949, when he joined FAO as a fisheries biologist. Here was a person well trained in the modern science of fish production.

When Dr. Lin arrived in Haiti he sought the answers to numerous questions. Were there any domestic fish that could be used for profitable farming? If not, what fish might be imported? Did the fresh-water systems, such as rivers, lend themselves to fish farming? What land area might be used for the construction of fish ponds? Might the rice fields be used? What kind of fish food was available? Was the climate of Haiti suitable for fish farming? Could the farmers be interested in raising fish? Could the skills and techniques of fish farming be easily learned?

After careful consideration of these matters, Dr. Lin was convinced that Professor Thompson had been correct in his suggestion that fish farming might be a part of the solution to Haiti's food problem. After consultation with officials of the Haitian government, Dr. Lin forwarded the results of his survey to the Fisheries Division at FAO Headquarters in Rome. Here other fisheries experts appraised the report and drafted a tentative plan for action. This plan was then submitted to the Inter-Divisional Group, which is composed of representatives of the five major Divisions of FAO: Forestry, Nutrition, Agriculture, Economics and Fisheries. This afforded an opportunity to get a many-sided view of the project based upon experiences gathered from all parts of the globe. After modifications had been made, the Fisheries Division drew up a formal working agreement which was presented to Dr. F. T. Wahlen, at that time Chief of the FAO Expanded Technical Assistance Program (*see Chapter 13*), as well as Director of FAO's Agriculture Division, for approval and submission to the government of Haiti.

Under this first agreement the Haitian government was to provide a 1950-1951 budget of 50,000 *gourdes* ($10,000) to cover expenses in Haiti, such as the building of ponds, the purchase of equipment, and travel costs within the country. Dr. Lin's salary, allowances, and traveling expenses outside Haiti were to be paid by FAO from United Nations Technical Assistance Program funds. This mutual program was approved by the government of Haiti, thus beginning the second part of the action suggested by Professor Thompson in 1948.

Dr. Lin then set about constructing a fish-farming program in three steps. In the first place, it was necessary to build a fish-fry nursery with a few experimental ponds to determine what fish would offer most in the way of production. After a supply of fish fry was established, he planned to develop demonstration and extension centers throughout Haiti where farmers could be schooled in fish culture. Lastly, attention was to be given to the marketing and use of fish, so that farmers might be offered an incentive to engage in fish farming.

By early 1951, enough experimental ponds had been established so that Dr. Lin and his assistant could determine what fish would be best suited to Haitian waters. In February and September 1951, a total of 420 carp fingerlings were introduced into the ponds from a hatchery in Alabama. In July of the same year 103 *Tilapia* were imported from Jamaica in the British West Indies. Both types of fish have shown remarkable growth, and their offspring are even now furnishing food for the people of Haiti. But if planting an acre of fish seemed to indicate the beginning of an American-style fish tale, this is nothing when compared with the story of how the *Tilapia* came to arrive in Haiti!

BACK IN 1939 Mr. W. H. Schuster, now of FAO, was visiting a fish farm in Indonesia. The farmer was pointing out some fingerlings he had raised in his fish pond. Although Mr. Schuster had spent many years in fishery work in Indonesia, he had never seen anything quite like them. While he was observing them, one of the fish released young fry from its mouth, as did several others that had been placed in a bucket by the farmer. Mr. Schuster realized that these must be mouth-breeding fish, a type of fish which protects eggs and young by guarding them in the mouth during the incubation period and moments of danger. But no fish of this type were known in Indonesia! Research determined that these were *Tilapia*, and of the type native to the inland waters of Mozambique, East Africa! The farmer declared he had found them in a small lagoon. No others were ever found. To this day there is no explanation of how these fish happened to be found thousands of miles from their home waters.

Whatever the *Tilapia* mystery might be, the important thing was that here were fish ideally suited to pond farming. Many fresh-water fish will spawn only in running water, in lakes, or in special breeding ponds. This means that fish ponds must be stocked each year from fry caught in natural waters or raised in hatcheries, a time-consuming and expensive process. Not so the *Tilapia!* They will breed in stagnant pond water as well as in free-running streams.

Fry from the original types were introduced into other ponds in Indonesia. They soon became the most popular pond fish. It wasn't long before the *Tilapia* were being raised on fish farms in Malaya, and it was from this latter region that they were brought to Jamaica in 1950 and then on to Haiti in 1951.

Having discovered several types of fish that would thrive in Haiti, Dr. Lin then turned to demonstrating methods of fish culture to the farmers of the island. An example of one farmer's interest is best expressed in Dr. Lin's own words:

For instance, there is a farmer in Damien who was in- spired by the ponds I built there and the fish raised in them. He asked me in April 1951 to advise him how to build a small pond in his farm, which I did. He immediately began

A balanced diet of fish and rice has been harvested from the pond shown in the background.

Workmen are shown deepening an already existing pond in Haiti.

Lin supervises the transporting arp and "Tilapia" fingerlings in -gallon cans.

"Tilapia" fingerlings imported from Jamaica are placed in ponds in Haiti.

Sure that no danger threatens, a "Tilapia" releases the amazing number of young fish it has been guarding in its mouth.

Studying the comparative value of various types of artificial fish food.

work, but it took him almost fourteen months to complete
that little pond of 1200 square feet in area and two feet
deep in water. It is now stocked with *Tilapia*, which are very
prolific and easy to raise. Though the yield of the small
pond will not be large, yet the zeal and effort made by the
farmer is admirable.

However small the yield may be, this farmer will always have a con-
venient, fresh supply of high-protein fish to supplement his diet. The
will and stamina of this one farmer is indicative of the way in which
people help themselves when human goodness and example point the
way.

By the middle of 1951 it became apparent that fish farming
in Haiti was well started. Equally important, however, to the long-
range program was the training of Haitian citizens themselves in
fish culture, as suggested in Professor Thompson's report. From September to November 1951, Mr. Leonce Bonnefil, Jr., Chief of the
Zoology Section of the Department of Agriculture, studied pond and
rice-field fish culture in Java under a fellowship provided by FAO.
In October and November of 1952, Mr. Emmanuel Garnier, Fisheries
Officer of the Department of National Economy, went to Brazil and
Surinam on another FAO fellowship there to study fish culture. The
knowledge these officials have gained means that eventually the work
can be handed over completely to Haitian citizens. Thus by the
beginning of 1953 the paper report of 1948 was a working reality!
—a reality that means more and better food for much of Haiti.

Other neighborhoods throughout the world are taking advantage
of this typical way in which FAO helps people to help themselves. Fish-
farming projects are in operation in such widely separated places as
Thailand, India, Iraq, and Israel—where it is hoped that fish production in Lake Tiberias (the Sea of Galilee) can be improved.
These are just a few of the lands where FAO is showing the advan-
tages that can come from combining traditional experience with

laboratory knowledge and applied science; is proving that the skill of one neighborhood can be extended to another; and is illustrating that "know-how" is not a monopoly of the more highly developed neighborhoods of the world.

Planting acres of fish is a skill now known to the many rather than the few. While this is but a small part of FAO's work, it demonstrates that harmonizing the will of people, the intelligence of governments, and the facilities of international organizations, neighborhoods can eventually eliminate that most persistent of all stumbling blocks to peace—hunger.

FOOD AND AGRICULTURE ORGANIZATION OF THE UNITED NATIONS: FAO

International Headquarters: Viale delle Terme di Caracalla, Rome, Italy

Origin

In May 1943 a United Nations Conference on Food and Agriculture met at Hot Springs, Virginia. Forty-four nations had accepted President Franklin D. Roosevelt's invitation to send representatives to this meeting. The delegates found themselves in agreement on certain basic points that later became the basis of FAO policy. Some of these were:

> The world has never had enough to eat. At least two-thirds of its people are ill-nourished in spite of the fact that two-thirds of the world's people are farmers.
>
> The modern science of nutrition proves beyond doubt that if all people could get enough of the right kinds of foods, the average level of health and well-being could be raised much higher than it is now.
>
> The modern science of production shows that it is entirely possible to produce enough of the right kinds of foods.

But production alone is not enough. Foods must be so distributed that the levels of consumption of those who do not have enough are progressively raised.

This implies an expanding world economy, in which each nation will play its own part, but all will act together.

The Hot Springs Conference recommended the establishment of the United Nations Interim Commission on Food and Agriculture to draft the plans for a permanent international organization whose purpose would be to work for the common objectives outlined above. The Interim Commission was set up in Washington, D. C., where a Constitution was drafted. After twenty of the forty-five nations eligible for original membership had informed the Interim Commission of their intention of joining a permanent organization, the first session of the FAO Conference was convened at Quebec, Canada, in October 1945.

Forty-two nations became charter members of FAO, which was the first of the new Specialized Agencies created after the end of World War II. Seldom before had so many nations joined together in a common effort to improve the lot of peoples throughout the world.

Purpose

The purpose of the FAO is stated in the Preamble to the Constitution, which reads as follows:

The Nations accepting this Constitution, being determined to promote the common welfare by furthering separate and collective action on their part for the purposes of

raising levels of nutrition and standards of living of the peoples under their respective jurisdictions,

securing improvements in the efficiency of the production and distribution of all food and agricultural products, bettering the condition of rural populations,

and thus contributing toward an expanding world economy,

hereby establish the Food and Agriculture Organization of the United Nations, hereinafter referred to as the "organization," through which the Members will report to one another on the measures taken and the progress achieved in the fields of action set forth above.

Functions

Article 1 of the Constitution describes the functions of FAO as follows:

1. The Organization shall collect, analyze, interpret, and disseminate information relating to nutrition, food, and agriculture. In this Constitution, the term "agriculture" and its derivatives include fisheries, marine products, forestry and primary forestry products.

2. The Organization shall promote and, where appropriate, shall recommend national and international action with respect to

a. scientific, technological, social, and economic research relating to nutrition, food, and agriculture;

b. the improvement of education and administration relating to nutrition, food, and agriculture, and the spread of public knowledge of nutritional and agricultural science and practice;

c. the conservation of natural resources and the adoption of improved methods of agricultural production;

d. the improvement of the processing, marketing, and distribution of food and agricultural products;

e. the adoption of policies for the provision of adequate agricultural credit, national and international;

f. the adoption of international policies with respect to agricultural commodity arrangements.

3. It shall also be the function of the Organization

a. to furnish such technical assistance as governments may request;

b. to organize, in cooperation with the governments concerned, such missions as may be needed to assist them to fulfill the obligations arising from their acceptance of the recommendations of the United Nations Conference on Food and Agriculture and of this Constitution; and

c. generally to take all necessary and appropriate action to implement the purposes of the Organization as set forth in the Preamble.

Membership

New members may be admitted to FAO by a two-thirds majority of the Conference, provided that a majority of the membership of the Organization is present. By May 1, 1954 there were seventy-one members of FAO. A listing of members appears in the Appendix.

Upon joining FAO, member nations assume certain obligations to the Organization. Among these are the submitting of reports and information relating to the purposes of the Organization; contributing to the budget as determined by the Conference; according immunities to staff members in so far as necessary to facilitate their work; maintaining membership for at least four years before giving notice of withdrawal from the Organization, which becomes effective a year following notification of this act to the Director-General.

Structure and Organization

FAO is operated by a Conference, a Council of the Food and Agriculture Organization, and the Director-General and his staff.

THE CONFERENCE

The Conference is the policy-making body of FAO, and is composed of one representative from each member nation. Each nation has one vote in the Conference, which provides means for member governments to get together biennially to review the world situation in food and agriculture, forestry and fisheries, discuss common problems, and agree on common action.

THE COUNCIL

Between sessions of the Conference, the eighteen-nation Council of FAO (also known as the World Food Council) keeps the world food and agriculture situation under constant review and makes whatever recommendations it considers necessary to member governments, international commodity authorities, and other specialized international agencies.

THE SECRETARIAT

The working staff of FAO is headed by a Director-General chosen by the Conference. Subject to the general supervision of the Conference and the Council, the Director-General has full power to direct the work of the Organization.

Five technical divisions of FAO have been established to deal with program operations: Agriculture, Forestry and Forest Products, Fisheries, Nutrition, and Economics. These divisions provide a wide range of fact-finding and advisory services designed to furnish information as the basis for national and international action on the related problems of food and agriculture. An Administrative Division provides services to the other divisions on budget, personnel, and similar matters.

Five regional offices have been established to serve as centers for the exchange of information, technical assistance, and encouragement to member governments to act together to solve special problems of their regions. The Near East Regional Office is in Cairo, Egypt; that for Asia and the Far East in Bangkok, Thailand. The North American Regional Office is at 1325 C Street, S. W., Washington, D. C. There are four smaller offices in Latin America, situated in Rio de Janeiro, Mexico City, Santiago and San José (Costa Rica).

The staff of FAO includes specialists and professional workers recruited from member countries. In addition to the headquarters staff, there are small staffs of technical officers in the regional offices and a number of technical experts working on specific projects in member countries. The importance of attracting competent people into the FAO and other international organizations was emphasized by Sir Herbert Broadley, Deputy Director-General of FAO, in a speech delivered at Rome in 1952:

> I believe that today we need more of these inspired leaders inside the team than we do the outstanding individualists. In FAO we are trying to help the backward countries of the world to achieve higher standards of living —more food, better clothes, more comfortable homes. Our greatest problem is to find the trained and inspired people who can carry out this work—modestly, efficiently and in close contact with the people of the country concerned. The world is desperately short of these trained people who can do this job. The work is not spectacular. It does not result in a Roman triumph with processions of captives and mountains of loot. Different from the conquests of old which turned prosperous cities and rich lands into deserts, this new crusade leaves behind deserts turned into culti-

vated land, waving fields of wheat, barley and corn, instead of marsh and jungle; more cows, sheep and pigs, orchards heavy with fruit, and forests changing bare hillsides into the very source of life.

We believe that it is only through international effort that these results can be achieved. Nations cannot any longer solve their problems alone. They are now too much dependent on each other. That is why we feel that FAO and the other parts of the United Nations have such an important work to undertake at the present time. Here is the field in which leadership as a member of the team awaits all the recruits the world can supply.

Activities

The work of FAO literally girdles the earth. The main drive is toward the full utilization of the basic soil and water resources of the world, particularly in underdeveloped countries. For this latter purpose FAO participates in the United Nations Expanded Program of Technical Assistance. In addition, FAO is encouraging member governments to establish a stable plan for the international exchange of agricultural products among the neighborhoods of the world. The examples of FAO activities that follow are but a small part of the total working program.

Experts have been invited into Afghanistan to undertake the control of sheep pox and the fostering of the Karakul sheep industry so important to the economy of that country. An FAO Veterinary Mission is helping Ethiopia to eliminate the dread cattle disease of rinderpest, while other missions are at work in Burma to stall the ravages of poultry diseases and in Egypt to control damages done by the cotton-leaf worm. Specialists are in British Guiana to study the possibility of utilizing unproductive land for cattle grazing, in Ceylon to demonstrate dry-farming methods, and in Ecuador to solve grain-storage and transportation problems.

In India two FAO experts are assisting in the maintenance and servicing of tractors and other equipment used in clearing and reclaiming land. In North Borneo a survey is being made of lands never used for agriculture. Soil maps are being drawn of these areas along with recommendations for suitable crops. FAO irrigation engineers are helping Iran to develop unused water resources, and soil-conservation projects are taking place in Jamaica. In one of the most densely populated sections of Pakistan an FAO specialist in land and water development is studying ways of forestalling recurring famines. FAO is helping to develop government research and extension service in the Philippines, and twelve specialists are implementing the work of the Agricultural Institute sponsored by the government of Saudi Arabia.

Forestry experts are in Austria making recommendations for reforestation, roads and cableways for logging, and the establishment of a sawmilling school. Others are in Brazil studying the means whereby one of the greatest forest reserves in the world, along the Amazon, may be opened. Chile and Paraguay are getting FAO assistance in forestry research and the establishment of forest services and schools. An FAO Forestry Mission of six experts is investigating various aspects of the Mexican lumbering industry. The pulp and paper industry of Thailand is under survey, and nine short-term experts are in Yugoslavia, where, among other things, they are suggesting uses for forest products that now go to waste.

Fisheries experts have been requested by Chile to make recommendations for the distribution, storage, marketing and popularization of fish. Other FAO personnel are suggesting means for developing the fishery resources in West Bengal, India, and along the coastal areas of East Pakistan. Specialists are in Turkey demonstrating proven methods for handling and processing fish.

FAO nutrition experts are organizing dietary surveys in Ecuador and training local nutritionists to carry them out. Greece requested

FAO help to assist in the improvement of the supply of milk, and India asked for aid in preserving and distributing this same commodity. In Indonesia, FAO is cooperating in the establishment of a National Nutritional Council. An FAO staff member studied ways of improving the diet of children in Portugal, and in Syria a home economics expert ran a successful Home Economics Workshop attended by teachers who received training in nutrition, child care, housing, and the management of nursery schools.

Regional training centers sponsored by governments and FAO have been set up to furnish technical assistance for the discussion of problems common to many countries in an area. These have concerned problems in nutrition, forest research, census tabulation, fisheries, control of locusts, and agricultural statistics. One such group sponsored by FAO, representing fourteen nations, toured the United States to study the prevention and control of forest fires.

Over and above these day-by-day activities of FAO, the Organization is giving careful consideration to the implementation of the Economic and Social Council's unanimous resolution of 1952 to provide immediate and effective aid to nations struck by famine. In December of 1951, the Council of FAO had invited the attention of the Economic and Social Council to the importance of making advance preparations for prompt action in such cases. In the resulting resolution, FAO was called upon to develop techniques for detecting famine emergencies and for estimating their duration. In addition, FAO was charged with the responsibility of notifying the Secretary-General of the United Nations when famine conditions existed.

Accordingly, FAO has established a monitorial system among its field workers so that they may immediately alert FAO headquarters if conditions in the country where they are working indicate that famine conditions may be imminent. A Committee of Experts appointed by the FAO Council is also studying the pros and cons of establishing a world food reserve to be used in such emergencies.

Thus FAO's activities range all the way from the little fish pond built by Dr. Lin's friend in Haiti to plans for the mobilization of the resources of the great nations. But whether the project be great or small, each is devoted to helping the neighborhoods of the world help themselves to a just share of goods and services.

National FAO Committees

Realizing that the action necessary to achieve the aims of FAO must be taken in member countries, the Director-General has invited member governments to establish FAO National Committees. Although each government must determine for itself whether such a Committee will be established, and if so what its functions will be, there has been general agreement that the following services are appropriate to such a Committee:

1. Preparation of the annual progress and program report;
2. Provision of answers to inquiries made by FAO;
3. Preparation of material for the national delegation to FAO conferences and meetings;
4. Liaison with non-governmental national organizations and institutions concerned with the work of FAO;
5. Dissemination of information about FAO;
6. Reception of and assistance to technical missions and individual officers sent to the country by FAO;
7. Assisting FAO to establish contact with scientific workers and technical experts;
8. Ensuring that the government makes the fullest possible use of the services of FAO and furnishes the Organization with any available material that may be useful for its work.

The United States has formed what is known as the FAO Interagency Committee to meet the needs outlined above. This Com-

mittee, consisting of twenty-three members, has its Headquarters in
the Office of Foreign Agricultural Relations at the Department of
Agriculture in Washington.

FLIGHT NINE SIXTY

International Civil Aviation Organization

THE FIRST COMMERCIAL INTERNATIONAL AIR SERVICE was established between London and Paris in 1919. This was but a scant sixteen years after the Wright brothers had made their first historic flights at Kitty Hawk, North Carolina. It was only natural that, because of the short distances between important trading centers of different countries in Europe, international air services should have had their beginning there. This system gradually expanded as airlines sought to link the countries of Europe with their colonies, and as they saw business opportunity in transferring people and goods from one neighborhood to another.

By the late 1920's and early 1930's British airlines were operating out of London down to the Middle East, from whence they branched either toward South Africa or on east to Australia. French air service linked Paris to Indo-China in the Far East and to Dakar in Africa. From this latter point the French lines crossed the Atlantic to Brazil. KLM (Royal Dutch) Airlines was providing like services to the Dutch colonies. In the same era Deutsche Lufthansa (German Airlines) was flying commercial planes through Africa and across the South Atlantic to Argentina. The first major United States concern to engage in international transport was Pan American Airways, which began a service in the Caribbean area in 1927.

By 1939 there were more than half a million miles of international air routes linking the major regions of the world. Although this marked a rapid advance in aircraft communication, the carrying of passengers and freight by air was but a small fraction of total international transport. World War II, which began in this same year, had a terrific impact upon air transport. Large military networks were built up around the civilian services. During six years of war, 27,000 aircraft were flown from North America to the combat areas of the world by the Royal Air Force Transport Command alone!

While the Royal Air Force Transport Command was the first such organization to be established, it was soon followed by the United States Army Air Transport Command and the United States Navy Air Transport Service. Together these services created a trail of air routes and landing fields across the globe. Much of the success enjoyed by these organizations can be traced to the skills acquired through civilian operations before the war.

These military operations not only made air transport a major factor in the exchange of goods and services throughout the world in wartime; they showed the enormous potential of air transport in a peacetime economy. This potential is being realized. The volume of air passenger traffic in 1952 was more than two and a half times that of 1946. In the same period, world air cargo traffic has increased more than fivefold.

Obviously this rapid development of international flying presents some very real problems. First are the technical problems of developing uniform operating procedures. Airlines of eleven different nations have scheduled flights to and from the New York International Airport at Idlewild. One can well imagine the confusion and danger that would exist without international cooperation to standardize operations! Less obvious, but equally important, are the economic and political problems that must be solved in regulating the movements of peoples, goods and services between neighborhoods.

To solve these specialized problems, sixty-two nations have banded themselves together in the International Civil Aviation Organization (ICAO) with headquarters in Montreal, Canada. Although not all nations in which airlines operate are members of ICAO, member nations account for over 95 per cent of all commercial international air transport. Some of the problems which ICAO has solved by gaining the cooperative consent of member nations become apparent when one looks behind the scenes as Trans World Airlines Flight Nine Sixty is completed from the New York International Airport to London.

Flight Nine Sixty leaves New York at five o'clock in the afternoon each Tuesday, and flies nonstop to arrive in London at quarter past eleven Wednesday morning (5:15 A.M. New York time). To many passengers this is a routine way of getting between neighborhoods; they give as little thought to how the plane gets to London as most of us do to the route of the train that takes us to visit relatives. But back of this flight is a very real example of teamwork—involving individuals, companies, governments and, finally, ICAO.

The pilot arrives at the airport two hours before flight time. He is joined there by the nine other members of the crew; two copilots, two flight engineers, the navigator, the radio operator, a hostess and two pursers. Each member of the crew is a specialist in a particular field. Each has met licensing standards established by ICAO. These specify the requirements as to training, experience, and physical condition that all members of the flight crew must meet. Requirements have also been set for those people engaged in ground occupations connected with aircraft operations.

After checking in the crew, the pilot, with his copilots and the navigator, confer with the TWA dispatcher. The dispatcher gives the pilot a list of the passengers and the cargo. He has also drafted a flight plan based upon the cargo weight and the latest weather reports. After the plan has been checked through, the airplane is taxied from the hangar to its assigned location at the terminal. Here the food for the trip is placed aboard, and the airplane is fueled.

On this particular flight, five thousand two hundred gallons of gasoline have been allowed. Under normal conditions a TWA Constellation will use four thousand gallons of fuel on the New York-London flight. ICAO requires that sufficient additional gasoline be carried to insure an adequate fuel reserve if the plane is forced to fly beyond its destination because of bad weather conditions or unexpected head winds. In this case, the extra twelve hundred gallons means that, should Flight Nine Sixty have to land at Paris because of conditions in London, the pilot, after using three hundred gallons to fly to Paris, would *still* have a reserve of three hours' flying time.

In the meantime the pilot has been going over the plane's equipment. He checks the fire extinguishers, the life rafts, the hand-powered radio, the evacuation chute, the emergency lights, and dozens of other items specified by ICAO's "Standards on Search and Rescue." These not only enumerate the items a plane must carry, but also set up procedures that are to be used should the plane be forced down en route. Detailed plans based upon the experiences of many years in coping with disasters are published in manuals known to ship captains as well as to pilots. They include instructions for reporting difficulties, techniques for ditching and open-sea landing, search plans for both aircraft and rescue boats, suggestions for locating survivors, instructions for survivors, details on dropping supplies, and the training of rescue crews.

Unaware of these elaborate precautions being taken to safeguard their journey, the passengers have been boarding the plane. Before joining them the pilot signs out with the customs, immigration, and public health officials assigned to the airport. In recent years ICAO has had considerable success getting national governments to cut down on the number of forms that must be completed before a plane may clear an international airport. Agreements now in effect among certain ICAO members lay down the maximum number of formalities that any country may require, thus simplifying the

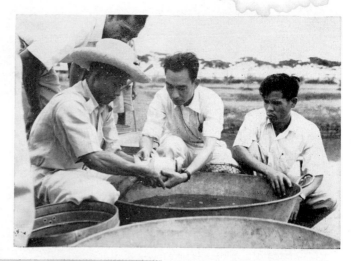

FAO expert working with the fisheries officers of Bangkhen Fisheries Station on the selection of breeders. Fish shown is the common carp, a popular pond fish.

Homeward bound after a hard day's work in the fish ponds.

Packing fish fingerlings in specially constructed oxygen supply containers for long-distance transport.

"Takeoff?"

A well coordinated system of communication is essential for safe and efficient airways operation across the North Atlantic.

"Each member of the crew is a specialis a particular field."

The U. S. Coast Guard Cutter "Spencer" is a 2300-ton turbine-powered vessel, built for patrolling and assigned to ICAO weather ship duty.

As trans-Atlantic planes approach the "Spencer" the radar operator traces their courses on the twin screens.

A radioman aboard the "Spencer" talks with the pilot of a passing plane, relaying weather information and data on the ship's position for navigational use. Latest weather data are posted on the illuminated circular chart (left) for relay.

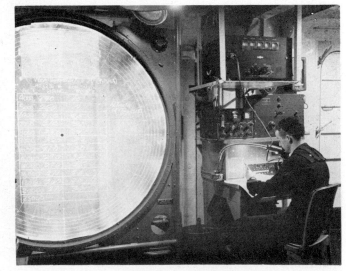

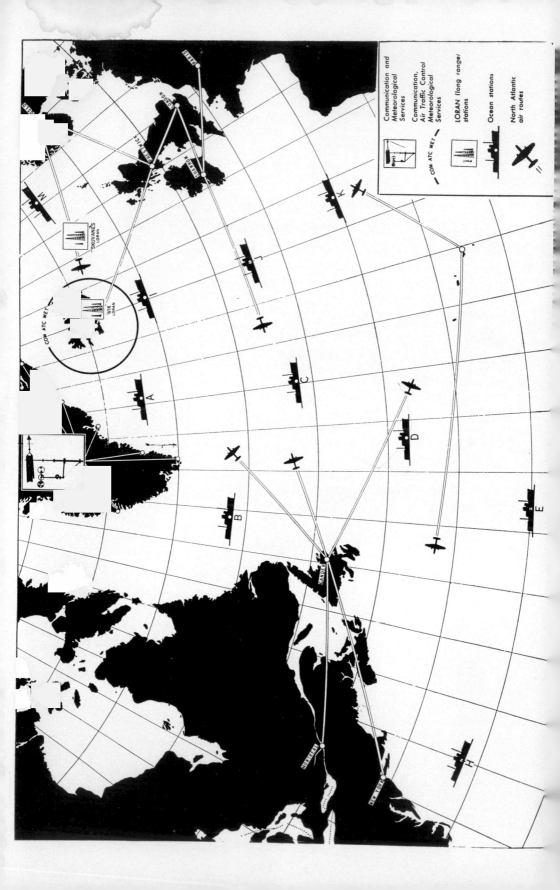

Communication and
Meteorological
Services

Communication,
Air Traffic Control
Meteorological
Services

LORAN (long range)
stations

Ocean stations

North Atlantic
air routes

paper work which airlines and airline crews must go through, and cutting down the waiting time for passengers.

Boarding the plane, the pilot rechecks the passenger list with the purser. Then he and his copilot double check a long list of items as a final precaution. Shortly before five the pilot receives permission from the control tower to taxi the plane to the head of the runway. There full power is turned into the engines as pilots and engineers search their instrument panels for the slightest indication of trouble. Sensing no difficulties, they are all set to receive final clearance from the tower: "TWA Nine Sixty, cleared to London Airport, cross Fire Island climbing, Nantucket nineteen thousand, maintain nineteen thousand via Nantucket, Yarmouth, then Pressure Pattern to London." The power is increased as the big plane roars down the runway and gently pulls off. The plane is airborne at 5:08 P.M. New York time.

From this point on, all references to time will be that of "Z" time figured on the twenty-four-hour clock to coincide with the time at the Greenwich meridian. Because of the vast number of time zones and the large number of dimensional units in use throughout the world, care must be taken so that there be no confusion in air-to-ground communications. One of the dimensional units specified by ICAO is Greenwich mean time. "Z" time is five hours ahead of Eastern Standard Time; thus, the official take-off time was 1008Z.

Fifty minutes after take-off, the plane is over Nantucket Island and has reached its airways cruising altitude of nineteen thousand feet. Airways traffic control and area traffic control are regulated by standards established by ICAO. Both horizontal and vertical flight lanes are set up. Planes flying from New York to London travel at the odd-numbered thousands of feet; those flying in the opposite direction, from London to New York, use the even-numbered levels. Only by such controls on the "superhighway of the air" can the constant flow of traffic between America and Europe be maintained safely and economically.

Five hours out of New York, Flight Nine Sixty is over Yarmouth, Nova Scotia, and shortly thereafter passes off to the right of Sydney, Nova Scotia. The lights of Sydney are the last signs of land this flight will have until the coast of Ireland shows up. All this time, and all the way to London, the flight is in constant touch with ground and ocean stations either by voice or code. Radio telephone can be used by Flight Nine Sixty under most conditions. But voice doesn't always get through, and when that happens the radio operator punches out the code on his key transmitter. The telecommunications network that keeps aircraft in touch with these stations and with other aircraft is the creation of ICAO. Working with the International Telecommunication Union (*Chapter 6*) ICAO assigns wave lengths for both mobile and fixed aeronautical radio services. ICAO is also responsible for arrangements made to broadcast weather information by special codes, and cooperates with the World Meteorological Organization (*Chapter 10*) in coordinating the reports received from thousands of weather-reporting facilities both on land and at sea.

When Flight Nine Sixty is some one hundred and twenty miles south of Torbay Field at St. John's, Newfoundland, the traffic control center at Moncton, New Brunswick, directs the pilot to descend to seventeen thousand feet. Air traffic ahead of Nine Sixty has priority on the higher altitudes, and is heavy enough so that this safety measure is taken even though all planes at the higher altitude are also flying east.

At least once each hour position reports are made to land and ocean stations so that air traffic can be regulated—and so rescue units will have this information for their operations if the plane stops checking in. In addition, pilots report when they are over designated spots established by air traffic controllers as check points through which all planes must enter and leave. These check points are indicated on the New York-London flight map at the intersections of certain agreed-upon degrees and minutes north, and degrees and minutes west. Flight Nine Sixty checks in over "Shark" intersection, located 49° 40′ N and 51° 30′ W. As a further safety precaution, twice each hour the radio operator tunes in at 500 kilocycles for three minutes. This is the international distress frequency to which all ships and planes throughout the world are tuned at the same time, with their operators listening for S O S—three dots, three dashes, three dots— the international distress signal.

Over the three thousand miles of water between North America and Europe, Flight Nine Sixty must have constant reports on the weather. The North Atlantic is one of the most unpredictable weather areas on earth, and without accurate information as to winds and storms, air travel over the New York-to-London route would be extremely dangerous. ICAO has solved this problem through the establishment of a network of nine ocean weather stations jointly maintained and financed by twelve nations whose planes cross this much-traveled region.

Each weather station usually involves two ships—one ship on station and one ship on reserve. Latitude 51° 45′ N and longitude 35° 30′ W marks the weather station "c for Coca," one of several that serve Flight Nine Sixty. Hour after hour, for weeks at a time, a United States Coast Guard ship cruises about in a few square miles of North Atlantic water. Every three hours the weather men record the surface weather conditions, and every six hours they make upper air observations. This latter is accomplished by releasing a helium-filled balloon to a height of sixty thousand feet. Delicate instruments attached to the balloon record the temperature, pressure, and humidity of the air through which it passes. These observations must be made in daylight and darkness and in all kinds of weather—tasks that demand the best in seamanship, courage, and skill.

The reports from the ocean weather stations make it possible to forecast weather conditions more accurately, and by so doing make travel across the Atlantic safer and more profitable. If an airlines dispatcher knows the weather conditions he can plot a course to take advantage of the wind, and when it is favorable he can reduce the fuel load and increase the passenger and freight load.

"Ocean Station Coca" has duties other than reporting weather conditions. The navigator aboard Flight Nine Sixty keeps his ADF (Automatic Direction Finder) tuned to Coca during the flight over Coca's area in order to check his course. Four times an hour for five minutes the homing facility (radio directional signal) operates from equipment aboard Coca and serves as a navigational checkpoint. The navigator may ask Coca for a "radar fix." This means he wants the radar operator aboard Coca to pick up the plane on his radar screen and to figure the plane's distance from the ship. As Coca's position varies but a few miles at any given time, this gives the navigator an opportunity to check his own calculations as to the plane's position.

In addition, the crew aboard Coca, and other weather ships, is equipped and trained to provide search and rescue assistance should a plane get into difficulties. Several years ago the flying boat *Bermuda Sky Queen,* bound from Ireland to Newfoundland, ran short of fuel and was forced to "ditch" in the North Atlantic. Following Coca's radio beacon, the large plane was able to come into the ocean almost beside the station. In spite of a high rolling sea the crew and passengers, numbering sixty-nine, were safely taken off the plane. A few weeks later the crew of a sinking Norwegian freighter was rescued by another weather ship operated by the British.

The passengers of Nine Sixty are sleeping, but below them in the night the small speck of white that is the weather ship continues its ceaseless plodding back and forth, providing unseen but unceasing service to the safety of the people above.

In addition to the weather ships, ICAO is responsible for other

joint support operations in the North Atlantic. These include meteorological and communications centers maintained in Greenland, Iceland, and the Faroe Islands. Safety for North Atlantic crossings makes
the establishment of these services essential. But it would not be fair
to ask the citizens of these lands to support financially a service
from which they derive but slight benefit. As a result ICAO has
worked out agreements whereby these installations are maintained
by the governments whose airlines use the facilities.

This same joint support applies to the LORAN (long range) stations in Iceland and the Faroe Islands that provide long-range
radio navigational aids for aircraft operating along the North Atlantic
route. These LORAN stations provide a fixed point of absolute de-
pendability for navigators. Under ordinary conditions the navigator
can best determine his exact position by a sextant shot of the sun during the day or of the stars at night. During rough weather these aids
are, of course, not available, although it is then that positional read-
ings are most important. While the weather ships can be used to advantage as fixing points, their position is never *exactly* known, and
during gales and storms they may actually be off their station and
not know too accurately where they are themselves.

The navigator remains busy all through the night. He combines
his own technical knowledge with the services provided by ICAO,
and the practical experience of many years, to keep the giant Constellation on its proper flight pattern. Shortly after 0930, his chart
shows Flight Nine Sixty to be some two hundred and ten miles off
the coast of Ireland. He relays this information to the captain. As
the radio operator's weather reports indicate all stations ahead are
clear, the plane continues past the southern tip of Ireland, winging
toward London Airport at a better than five-mile-a-minute clip.

The sky is overcast past Ireland, but shortly thereafter the clouds
become scattered and the passengers catch a glimpse of St. George's
Channel, which separates Ireland from England. Soon the dark out-

lines of the coast of Wales appear—a thrill to both passengers and crew.

Over Wales, direct voice contact is made with London Airport, and clearances and altitudes are given just as they were in New York yesterday afternoon. Over Bristol the descent from the seventeen-thousand-foot flight level is started, and by the time the plane is over Epsom Range station just south of the airport the altitude is down to twenty-five hundred feet. At this point London radar control takes over and "talks" Flight Nine Sixty in.

Whether the aircraft is landing by night or day, in fair weather or under conditions of very bad visibility, ICAO regulations make for perfect coordination between the pilot and the ground air traffic control. ICAO international standards on aerodromes specify the layout and design of airports and of approach lights. Agreement has been reached as to the pattern of high-intensity approach lights to guide an aircraft coming into the airport on an instrument-landing-system beam (ILS) or ground-controlled approach (GCA).

The London Director has lined Flight Nine Sixty up for a landing on runway ten, right. The pilot goes over his check list with other members of the crew and then orders the landing gear down. The great plane sinks lower and lower, and finally crosses over the approach lights. Suddenly the cement runway is reached, and the wheels touch down on London Airport. The plane is eleven hours and fifty-five minutes from New York—just seven minutes over the original flight plan!

Certainly Flight Nine Sixty can be viewed as a lesson in international cooperation. The International Civil Aviation Organization has played an important role in this flight. ICAO will play an ever more vital role in the orderly movement of peoples and goods between the neighborhoods of the world as peoples and governments work toward the ideals expressed in the "Five Freedoms of the Air":

1. The privilege of an airline of one country to fly across the territory of another country, without landing, en route to its final destination.
2. The privilege of an airline of one country to land in another country's territory for non-traffic purposes, such as refueling or engine repairs.
3. The privilege of an airline of one country to carry passengers, freight, and mail from a foreign country to its own.
4. The privilege of carrying passengers, freight, and mail from its own country to a foreign one.
5. The privilege of an airline of one country to carry passengers, freight, and mail between the airports of two foreign countries.

INTERNATIONAL CIVIL AVIATION ORGANIZATION: ICAO

International Headquarters: International Aviation Building, Montreal, Canada

Origin

The first international meeting to reach agreements on air flight was the Paris Peace Conference of 1919. The rapid advance in aircraft development during World War I had made possible the establishment of commercial air service. As has been noted, the first regularly scheduled air run between London and Paris was established in 1919, and focused the attention of the peacemakers upon this new method of international transportation.

Out of the Paris Conference came two important decisions. The first of these was the acknowledgment that the air space over each nation was owned by that nation. This meant that other nations wishing to fly planes into or over any other nation must first get permission. The second agreement led to the establishment of the

International Commission for Air Navigation (ICAN), an organization open to nations who wished to share in the technical improvement of aviation. Some of the major powers, including the United States, did not join ICAN. Nevertheless, ICAN was an important influence in the expansion of commercial air travel that took place between the two world wars.

The rapid development of air transport during World War II raised new technical, political, and economic problems that had to be solved for peacetime aviation. Realizing that the limited influence of ICAN would not be sufficient to cope with these new problems, the government of the United States extended invitations to fifty-five allied and neutral nations to meet in Chicago in November 1944 to discuss international air affairs.

For seven weeks the delegates of the fifty-two nations that accepted invitations to the Chicago Conference considered the problems of international civil aviation. Their decisions mark a great milestone in man's attempt to facilitate the exchange of goods and services between the neighborhoods of the world.

The delegates reaffirmed the Paris Peace Conference principle that each nation had absolute control of the air space over its territory. Upon this principle they drafted a Convention on International Civil Aviation consisting of ninety-six articles. This provided for the establishment of an International Civil Aviation Organization that was to come into existence thirty days after a minimum of twenty-six nations had ratified the Convention. The provisions of ratification stated that the governments concerned must approve the Convention as a treaty. As this is a time-consuming task, the Conference drafted an Interim Agreement on International Civil Aviation which established a temporary body known as the Provisional International Civil Aviation Organization (PICAO), with limited powers, to serve as an advisory group until the Convention might be approved.

By June 1945, twenty-six nations had signed the Interim Agreement, and PICAO was established in Montreal, Canada. For the twenty months of its existence, PICAO laid the foundations for an international organization designed to improve, facilitate, and co-ordinate air flight over national boundaries. Much of PICAO's work consisted in the drafting of recommendations for standards, practices, and procedures to achieve safe and efficient international flight. PICAO did its task well, and when, on April 4, 1947, thirty days after the twenty-sixth nation had ratified the Convention, ICAO came into being, it inherited a going organization.

Purposes

The purposes of the ICAO are clearly laid down in the Preamble to the Convention on International Civil Aviation:

Whereas the future development of international civil aviation can greatly help to create and preserve friendship and understanding among the nations and peoples of the world, yet its abuse can become a threat to the general security; and

Whereas it is desirable to avoid friction and to promote that cooperation between nations and peoples upon which the peace of the world depends;

Therefore, the undersigned governments having agreed on certain principles and arrangements in order that international civil aviation may be developed in a safe and orderly manner and that international air transport services may be established on the basis of equality of opportunity and operated soundly and economically;

Have accordingly concluded this Convention to that end.

Functions

ICAO's responsibilities are established in the Convention as follows:

Develop the principles and techniques of international air navigation and foster the planning and development of international air transport so as to:

Insure the safe and orderly growth of international civil aviation throughout the world;

Encourage the arts of aircraft design and operation for peaceful purposes;

Encourage the development of airways, airports, and air navigation facilities for international civil aviation;

Meet the needs of the peoples of the world for safe, regular, efficient, and economical air transport;

Prevent economic waste caused by unreasonable competition;

Insure that the rights of contracting states are fully respected and that every contracting state has a fair opportunity to operate international airlines;

Avoid discrimination between contracting states;

Promote safety of flight in international air navigation;

Promote generally the development of all aspects of international civil aeronautics.

Membership

As of May 1, 1954, sixty-two nations were members of ICAO. A listing of members appears in the Appendix.

Although the Chicago Conference that drafted the Convention met during the height of World War II, provisions were made for the later admission of Axis nations. These provisions called for an affirmative four-fifths vote of the Assembly and the approval of any member national that had been invaded or attacked during the war by the state seeking admission. Under these provisions, Italy and Japan have become members of ICAO.

Structure and Organization

ICAO is governed by an Assembly that in turn elects a Council to serve as the executive body. The administrative functions of the Organization are performed by the Secretariat, which makes up the third principal organ of ICAO.

THE ASSEMBLY

The ICAO Assembly governs the activities of the Organization. Each member nation has representation in the Assembly and each nation has one vote. Article 49 of the Convention established the powers and duties of the Assembly as follows:

> *a.* elect at each meeting its President and other officers; *b.* elect the contracting states to be represented on the Council; *c.* examine and take appropriate action on the report of the Council and decide on any matter referred to it by the Council; *d.* determine its own rules of procedure and establish such subsidiary commissions as it may consider to be necessary or desirable; *e.* vote an annual budget and determine the financial arrangement of the Organization; *f.* review expenditures and approve the accounts of the Organization; *g.* refer, at its discretion, to the Council, to subsidiary commissions, or to any other body any matter within its sphere of action; *h.* delegate to the Council the powers and authority necessary or desirable for the discharge of the duties of the Organization and revoke or modify the delegations of authority at any time; *i.* consider proposals for the modification or amendment of the provisions of this Convention and, if it approves of the pro-

posals, recommend them to the contracting states; *j.* deal with any matter within the sphere of action of the Organization not specifically assigned to the Council.

On October 30, 1947, following Assembly approval, ICAO formally entered into working relationship with the United Nations.

THE COUNCIL

The ICAO Council is a permanent body composed of twenty-one member nations elected by the Assembly for a term of three years and responsible to the Assembly. Council decisions require a majority vote. Member states, not members of the Council, may participate in Council proceedings (without voting) when the matter under discussion concerns the member's interest. Article 54 of the Convention lays down the following functions for the Council:

> *a.* submit annual reports to the Assembly; *b.* carry out the directions of the Assembly and discharge the duties and obligations which are laid on it by the Convention; *c.* determine its organization and rules of procedure; *d.* appoint and define the duties of an Air Transport Committee, which shall be chosen from among the representatives of the members of the Council, and which shall be responsible to it; *e.* administer the finances of the Organization; *f.* determine the emoluments of the President of the Council; *g.* appoint a chief executive officer who shall be called the Secretary-General, and make provision for the appointment of such other personnel as may be necessary; *h.* request, collect, examine, and publish information relating to the advancement of air navigation and the operation of international air services, including information about the costs of operation and particulars of subsidies paid to airlines from public funds; *i.* report to contracting states any infractions of the Convention, as well as any failure to carry out recommendations or determinations of the Council; *j.* report to

the Assembly any infraction of the Convention where a contracting state has failed to take appropriate action within a reasonable time after notice of the infraction; *k.* adopt international standards and recommended practices, and notify all contracting states of the action taken; *l.* consider recommendations of the Air Navigation Commission for amendment of the Annexes; *m.* consider any matter relating to the Convention which any contracting state refers to it.

Assisting the Council in carrying out its functions are special advisory bodies. The Air Navigation Commission makes recommendations concerning technical matters. This twelve-member body has drafted Annexes to the Convention on such matters as personnel licensing, rules of the air, and search and rescue, which the Council in turn has submitted to member nations for their guidance. The Air Transport Committee advises the Council on economic matters of importance to international flight, such as commercial rights, air mail, payments for airport facilities, and statistical reporting. The Committee on Joint Support of Air Navigation Services studies and reports to the Council on joint operations such as the ocean weather stations. The Legal Committee provides advice on public and private air law and drafts international agreements for ICAO.

THE SECRETARIAT

The administrative functions of ICAO are performed by the Secretariat under the direction of the Secretary-General, who is chosen by the Council. Made up of four bureaus (Air Navigation, Air Transport, Legal, Administration and Services) the Secretariat supplies technical and administrative aid to the various committees and divisions of the Council.

Personnel for the Secretariat are recruited on a wide geographical basis. Opportunities are provided to member nations so that they may send selected young men to the ICAO Secretariat for a period of training. Following this study, the trainees return to the employment of their governments and airlines better equipped to contribute to safe and efficient air transport in their own lands and with a realistic understanding of ICAO's spirit and purpose.

Activities

The activities of the International Civil Aviation Organization are as far-flung as the airways they help service. The ICAO world map is subdivided into ten major regions. On this map are pinpointed some forty thousand future facilities to be located or services to be rendered as they have been drafted at regional meetings. ICAO carries on constant study leading to the ways in which governments may be encouraged and helped to fill these gaps. Record books are kept that reflect the day-by-day progress that is being made toward fulfilling these world-wide plans.

Specific problems are brought to the attention of ICAO by organizations such as the International Air Transport Association. One such problem concerned the need for better coordination of civil and military air traffic in much-traveled Western Europe. Following a proposal of investigation submitted to ICAO by the Netherlands, the Council worked out plans for a special meeting to be held in Paris on this subject. With the cooperation of governments, airlines, and ICAO, agreements were reached that led to an improved, hence safer and more efficient, European airways system.

The wide use of jet-propelled aircraft and the increase in helicopter services create new problems in the fields of aerodrome construction and operating conditions. Many problems that were new several years ago have been solved and are matters of record in Annexes to the Convention. These include: standardization of radio aids to navigation, codifying instrument flight rules, and many communication procedures. Although ICAO actions are not binding upon any member government until that government formally adopts them, the wide use of ICAO's publications and the small number of rejections of parts of Annexes attest to the wide acceptance of ICAO decisions.

The increased use of voice communications raises serious problems, since pilots and control personnel must often use a language other than their own. ICAO has developed a new phonetic alphabet that can be pronounced by airmen of almost every nationality. The Alfa-Bravo-Coca alphabet is coming into wide acceptance and lessens the danger of misinterpretation, resulting in greater safety. Ocean Station Coca was known as "Charlie" under the old alphabet.

One of the most difficult fields of operation for ICAO has been that of simplifying the rules and regulations involved in moving an aircraft and its load across international boundaries. Over the last five years the time that passengers must spend in being cleared at an international airport has been cut by a third. Although much remains to be done to speed procedure, ICAO-recommended standards on unloading baggage, customs inspections, travel visas, landing cards, and passport controls have proved their worth when used by member governments. Even more pressing are the economic and political problems connected with "the privilege of an airline of one country to carry passengers, freight, and mail between the airports of two foreign countries"—the "fifth freedom." Thus far nations have not been able to agree upon solutions to these problems. ICAO's Council has made recommendations on the subject and stands ready to call future conferences when member governments so desire.

ICAO shares in the United Nations Technical Assistance Program. A major contribution of ICAO has been the training of local personnel in such fields as air transport control, communications, and aeronautical meteorology, when governments have so requested. Without this training, safe and efficient civil air operations are an impossibility.

A wide variety of other technical assistance programs have been undertaken: air transport surveys have been made in Afghanistan and El Salvador; advice on airport construction has been extended Indonesia, Israel, and Jordan; with ICAO assistance, Thailand and Turkey have organized government departments of civil aviation; Ethiopia and Jordan have received advice on drawing up aviation laws; an ICAO mission of seven experts made a thoroughgoing study of air transport problems and possibilities in Iran. More than thirteen governments requested the United Nations Technical Assistance Program to provide ICAO services in 1953.

Dr. Edward Warner, President of the Council of ICAO, has summarized the purpose behind ICAO's activities in the following words:

> ICAO is an association of national governments which have recognized the need for working together for the good of civil aviation and for the healthy development of international relationships. No one nation acting within its own territory and with its own resources could make its civil aviation as safe, as reliable, as economical, or as useful as it could be if that nation worked together with its neighbours. Not even the most powerful government on earth, sovereign over the widest territories, could do that. Recognition for the need of constant cooperation has brought most of the world into the ICAO membership. The same recognition will, I believe, convince the remaining states that they cannot long forego the benefits of membership.

Below deck, the course of an aircraft in distress over the open waters of the North Atlantic is charted by a crewman on a plotting board.

Trainees from various Member nations of ICAO participate in a demonstration of the new ILA language for aviation at ICAO Headquarters in Montreal.

e Council of the International il Aviation Organization at its adquarters in Montreal, Canada.

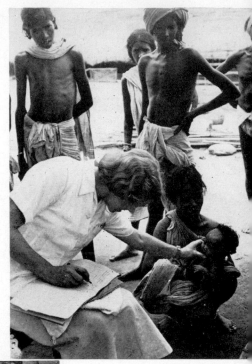

Mrs. Bille-Brahe keeps records of the health situation of mothers and children in a village in the WHO-UNICEF Malaria Control Team's area (Orissa, India).

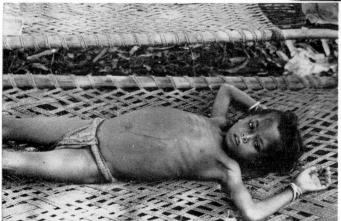

An enlarged spleen marks child as a malaria victim.

Here is Nurse Bille-Brahe at the bedside of a plague victim during an epidemic in a South Indian town.

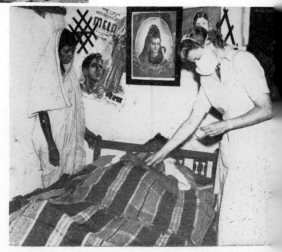

3

WHO

UNICEF

THE DIARY OF
MRS. BILLE-BRAHE

World Health Organization
United Nations Children's Fund

> *February 4:* Went along the main road to
> Edakkara, then turned left along a sandy path.
> Jeep was able to take us only two miles. From
> there we had to walk. The houses here are very
> scattered, often as much as a mile apart.

IF ONE HAD TO IDENTIFY the writer of these lines
unaided, it would prove quite difficult. Perhaps the extract is from
the diary of a military commander visiting his outposts at the front?
Or, these might be the notes of a surveyor on a field trip to spot the
route for a new highway. A fisherman seeking for out-of-the-way
streams in which to try his luck might record these words at the
end of the day's sport. One would never guess that this is actually
part of a diary kept by an attractive flaxen-haired young Danish
woman who was reporting a routine part of her duties as a nurse
from deep in the south of India!

The story of how the author of this diary, Mrs. Inga Bille-Brahe,
happened to be walking along a remote trail thousands of miles from
her native city of Copenhagen is one that involves governments, international organizations, and people of skill, patience, and good will.

The 350,000,000 people of India comprise one-sixth of the world's
population. Since 1947 India has been a free and independent nation.
Working through their democratic institutions, the peoples are re-

solved to seek a better future for themselves by attacking the allied problems of poverty, disease, and hardship.

Malaria is a wasting disease that has intensified hunger and hardship in India. Although it strikes people of all ages, it is particularly hard on children, who run a high fever and become too listless to play or study. Sometimes their stomachs become horribly swollen, while the rest of the body shrinks to extreme thinness. It is estimated that in 1944 alone more than two million Indians died of this disease. Aside from the suffering which is directly attributable to malaria, it adds to India's constant threat of famine; malaria-weakened farmers produce less food for themselves and others.

Government leaders in the new state of India realized that Western scientists and doctors had knowledge that could lead to the elimination of this scourge. Further, their government was a participating member in international organizations set up to tackle problems of this very nature. Accordingly, India petitioned for help in the form of World Health Organization and United Nations International Children's Emergency Fund (WHO/UNICEF) malaria-control teams.

For these teams WHO provided the technical personnel, while UNICEF furnished the supplies, equipment, and transport. The government of India assigned an understudy team of its own citizens and provided labor squads, foremen, mechanics, and chauffeurs.

As the public health nurse for one of these teams, WHO secured the services of Mrs. Bille-Brahe. A citizen of Denmark, she was a graduate of a nursing school, where she had specialized in surgical training. After registering with the Danish National Health Service in 1942, she continued her studies, this time concentrating on epidemic diseases and pediatrics. In 1949 she completed a public health nurse's course and in September of that year joined WHO. Her technical training made her an excellent choice for the WHO/UNICEF assignment, and in addition she possessed those qualities of patience, perseverance, and good will so essential for winning the confidence and cooperation of others.

After a period of training with a WHO/UNICEF malaria-control team already at work in Mysore State, Mrs. Bille-Brahe was assigned to join team-leader Dr. L. Mara, of Italy, who was opening an operation in India's Malabar District. The team's headquarters was in the city of Nilambur, from which it was to service a 236-square-mile area in which were hundreds of small villages.

Transportation to the villages presented some very real problems, as the following three entries in Mrs. Bille-Brahe's diary indicate:

February 2: Karakod is the farthest hamlet in Nilambur Taluk. The place can be reached only by walking for about two miles through the paddies. Altogether there are only seven houses in the village.

February 8: These three villages we reached by walking through the forest. Once we lost our way and spent two hours wandering about until we finally came across the houses that we were looking for.

February 28: Visited the hamlets of Meppad, Manthoni, and Punjoola. After crossing several streams the jeep was unable to go farther. These villages are situated just below the hills, and the houses are very scattered. The people are chiefly from the hill-tribes and some of them live only in tiny huts made of leaves. Oddly enough they were not shy or afraid, but came forward and talked frankly about their problems.

Many times on the first visit to the villages the people were quite frightened of meeting such queerly dressed strangers. The headman in each village had to be convinced of the reasoning behind the visit. Team members had to make the village leader understand that the mosquito is the carrier of malaria, and that DDT sprayed on the walls of the hut will kill the mosquito but will not harm the members of the family. It is the custom among some of the Mohammedans living in this area to whitewash the inside of their huts after a baby has been born. The mosquito will not die if the walls are whitewashed after the application of DDT. Getting the villagers to forego this important custom required many long hours of persuasion. But soon the teams were known throughout the area, and on the day of their expected arrival in a village people would walk for miles to greet them.

While the malariologists and entomologists went about their tasks of spraying DDT, examining patients, collecting and dissecting mosquitoes and larvae, and maintaining their scientific records, Mrs. Bille-Brahe made contact with the village people. She gave drugs to malaria sufferers, treated minor illnesses, and above all helped care for the health of the mothers and children.

Of course, at the same time we inquire about the health of the family and give suggestions on cleanliness, food, etc. We always ask about the food of the baby and try to help mothers understand the importance of carrying out a few simple rules concerning its feeding. The mothers are often ignorant about what kind of solid food is suitable for a child. The baby's resistance is thus likely to be reduced and it becomes an easy prey to different infectious diseases.

It is difficult to find a way of getting improvement in health through better food. Even a mother who is expecting a baby can't be expected to buy milk and eggs. These products are very expensive. The price of a goat, for instance, is much too high even for a schoolmaster. Unfortunately, even vegetables are difficult to get, and only a few families will have a kitchen garden.

The teams realized that many diseases were due to malnutrition.

They taught mothers the value of using limes in the family menu and convinced many of them that spinach can be fed to babies. Milk powder and cod-liver oil received from UNICEF through the government proved a blessing to many mothers, infants, and children.

When the parents proved reluctant toward the planting of kitchen gardens, Mrs. Bille-Brahe took her educational campaign into the schools.

March 6: Saw the headmaster of the school at Etekkare village. He promised to let the children make a kitchen garden near the school as soon as the rainy season starts. The schoolteachers everywhere are very kind and a good help. The children are sweet and attentive and very eager to carry out the small bits of advice that we give them.

The older children were asked to draw the plan for a kitchen garden. They found out what was best to sow in it. Some went to the market to find out the price of seed. Many have interested their parents in these projects.

The schools also provided a wonderful opportunity for valuable public health work.

March 7: Gave lesson No. 11 to the school children. Explained to the headmaster that we were going to start a laboratory examination for evidences of intestinal worms. He immediately promised all the help we wanted. On the way back we visited Tharisil village and gave a lesson on malaria in Manbata school.

Short, very simple talks for the small children. We draw a picture of a fly on the blackboard to count how many legs a fly has. So many flies with so many unwashed legs (a fly never washes its legs as an Indian child does!) come in from outside and sit on the food. What to do about it? The children find out themselves. "Cover the food with banana leaves!"

In addition to the village leaders and the schools it proved very important to get the cooperation of the village midwives. These women care for mothers who are expecting new babies and safeguard the children at the very start of their life. They always have the confidence of the entire village, and if they can be convinced of the WHO/UNICEF program the other residents can be won.

March 10: Many home visits were made, and due to the interest shown by the midwife we are expecting an improvement of antenatal and postnatal care in the future. We discussed the following items with this midwife: (1) keeping as a help for herself a brief diary which would make it easier for her to remember the questions she would like to talk over with us and to see whether advice given had been acted upon, etc.; (2) marking up the maternal cards more carefully.

By the end of March Mrs. Bille-Brahe had paid seven visits to the Kalikavu midwife, and the results are clearly reflected in her report for that month.

We are happy to state that she is not at all sorry for our visits even if it does mean that she has more work. She is eager to learn and her work has improved in many ways.

Trained midwives are few in number. To encourage their interest and improve their service, UNICEF has assembled medical kits for distribution to those in training and those in practice.

Work of this kind is not without its humor. After a few visits to the villages with the team, the Danish nurse and her native public health assistant, "the wonderful, sweet" Josephine Devasahayam, would return alone. The Indian women who had long wondered how it was possible for women to travel by themselves decided that Josephine was her daughter. As Mrs. Bille-Brahe was some ten years younger than her assistant, this didn't make her too happy. When she asked the village women how they discovered this relationship, they said innocently: "Why, little mother—you have white hair and so many wrinkles!"

The people in the villages had difficulty in pronouncing Mrs. Bille-Brahe's name, but she soon learned that her given name, Inga, was easily enunciated. She became affectionately known as "Mrs. Inga" to thousands of residents in the Malabar District. With her Indian assistant, "Mrs. Inga" visited nearly a hundred villages during the month of February alone.

Not every day was spent in the villages. During the month of March there are brief entries in the diary such as these: "Holiday; office work," or "Jeep under repair; office work," or "Office work— lack of petrol; a large number of patients came to the office for treatment." Near the end of the month a more detailed entry appears.

> *March 30:* Office work. A great number of dressings were made out of old rags, washed and boiled. They also have produced a great number of children's diapers, etc. We never fail to tell mothers how they themselves can prepare these things; but, of course, many will not be able to spare even old rags. It's then that we are happy to have our little stock.

Mrs. Bille-Brahe didn't mention the conditions under which she lived at the headquarters. Dr. Cecily Williams of the WHO Regional Office in New Delhi included the following comments after a visit to the WHO/UNICEF team: drinking water and all other water had to be carried from a well some distance away, and be boiled; there was no modern plumbing; no electricity, so that it was impossible to use fans even though the temperature went above one hundred; team members could not sleep outside, as many people do, because tigers had been seen prowling around not far from the bungalow!

Dr. Williams also recorded her observations of the results of the work performed by the public health nurses. Each village and school that had been regularly visited showed great improvement. The villages were neater and the housekeeping more efficient. The residents had better knowledge of hygiene and were aware of its importance for themselves and for their families. The confidence of the village people had been won, and with it the battle against malaria.

When a village has been freed of malaria, a new life begins for its people. More work can be done. Better crops can be harvested. Diets can be improved. Families no longer need fear that the dreaded disease will strike their children.

The importance of the contributions made by this and other WHO/UNICEF teams and their devoted members is reflected in the new hopes in the minds of people. Strong, healthy, and happy people will maintain and strengthen their democratic institutions. Their cause is the cause of freedom.

WORLD HEALTH ORGANIZATION: WHO

*International Headquarters: Palais des Nations,
Geneva, Switzerland*

Origin

The origin of the World Health Organization may be said to date from the proposal of the Brazilian delegation at the San Francisco Conference that the word "health" be included in the United Nations Charter. The subsequent decision of the Conference is included in Article 55 of the Charter, which states that the United Nations shall promote *health* as one of the "conditions of stability and well-being which are necessary for peaceful and friendly relations among nations. . . ." To insure cooperative future action, Brazil and China jointly appealed the Conference to provide for an international health conference.

This plea was met with dispatch by the Economic and Social Council at its first meeting in February 1946. ECOSOC named a Technical Preparatory Committee of sixteen experts who drafted an agenda and certain proposals for the first international health conference, which convened in New York City on June 19, 1946.

There the Constitution of the new World Health Organization was drafted and signed at its conclusion, July 22, 1946, by the representatives of sixty-one nations. On this same date these representatives signed an agreement setting up an Interim Commission of eighteen members charged with the responsibility of making preparations for the first Health Assembly, to be convened within six months after the twenty-sixth nation had formally approved the Constitution. Accordingly, on June 24, 1948, the representatives of most of the countries on earth met at Geneva, Switzerland, for the initial World Health Assembly. For the first time in history a single organization was mobilized to attack international problems of health.

Purposes

The purposes of the World Health Organization are set forth in the Preamble to its Constitution, the provisions of which ring sturdy challenges to the peoples and governments of the world.

Health is a state of complete physical, mental and social well-being and not merely the absence of disease or infirmity.

The enjoyment of the highest attainable standard of health is one of the fundamental rights of every human being without distinction of race, religion, political belief, economic or social condition.

The health of all peoples is fundamental to the attainment of peace and security and is dependent upon the fullest cooperation of individuals and States.

The achievement of any State in the promotion and protection of health is of value to all.

Unequal development in different countries in the promotion of health and control of disease, especially communicable disease, is a common danger.

Healthy development of the child is of basic importance; the ability to live harmoniously in a changing total environment is essential to such development.

The extension to all peoples of the benefits of medical, psychological and related knowledge is essential to the fullest attainment of health.

Informed opinion and active cooperation on the part of the public are of the utmost importance in the improvement of the health of the people.

Governments have a responsibility for the health of their peoples which can be fulfilled only by the provision of adequate health and social measures.

Functions

The functions of the World Health Organization are established in Chapter II of the Constitution. Those functions pertinent to the carrying out of such objectives as India's request for aid in eradicating malaria are as follows:

to act as the directing and coordinating authority on international health work;

to establish and maintain effective collaboration with the United Nations, specialized agencies, governmental health administrations, professional groups and such other organizations as may be deemed appropriate;

to assist governments, upon request, in strengthening health services;

to furnish appropriate technical assistance and, in emergencies, necessary aid upon the request or acceptance of governments; . . .

to stimulate and advance work to eradicate epidemic, endemic and other diseases; . . .

to promote, in cooperation with other specialized agencies where necessary, the improvement of nutrition, housing, sanitation, recreation, economic or working conditions and other aspects of environmental hygiene; . . .

to promote maternal and child health and welfare and to foster the ability to live harmoniously in a changing total environment; . . .

to promote improved standards of teaching and training in the health, medical and related professions; . . .

to assist in developing an informed public opinion among all peoples on matters of health.

Membership

Membership in WHO is open to all nations. Members of the United Nations may join by accepting the Constitution. Other nations may be admitted when their application has been approved by a simple majority of the Health Assembly. An interesting provision of the Constitution provides for the admission as associate

members of territories not responsible for the conduct of their own
international affairs, provided their representatives are qualified by
technical competence and that they come from the native population.

As of May 1, 1954, there were eighty-one members of WHO
(including those countries which have withdrawn) and three associate members. A detailed listing of WHO membership appears in
the Appendix.

In joining WHO, each member assumes certain responsibilities
of reporting to the Organization. These obligations are enumerated
in Chapter XIV of the Constitution.

> Each Member shall report annually to the Organization
> on the action taken and progress achieved in improving
> the health of its people.
>
> Each Member shall report annually on the action taken
> with respect to recommendations made to it by the Or-
> ganization and with respect to conventions, agreements and
> regulations.
>
> Each Member shall communicate promptly to the Organi-
> zation important laws, regulations, official reports and sta-
> tistics pertaining to health which have been published in
> the State concerned.
>
> Each Member shall provide statistical and epidemiological
> reports in a manner to be determined by the Health As-
> sembly.
>
> Each Member shall transmit upon the request of the
> Board such additional information pertaining to health as
> may be practicable.

Structure and Organization

The policies of WHO are determined by the World Health Assembly. The Executive Board serves as the organ for carrying out the policies agreed to by the Assembly. The administrative work of the Organization is accomplished by the Secretariat.

THE WORLD HEALTH ASSEMBLY

The World Health Assembly meets annually and is composed of delegates from member states, each of which has one vote. The assembly is empowered to adopt regulations necessary to carrying out the functions previously enumerated as necessary to attain the objectives of the Organization. The Assembly appoints the Director-General and names the members entitled to designate a person for the Executive Board. It also reviews and approves the WHO budget.

THE EXECUTIVE BOARD

The Executive Board consists of eighteen persons designated by as many member nations and chosen by the Assembly with due regard for geographical distribution. The Constitution requires that the Board meet at least twice a year, and empowers the Board to elect its own chairman. Members serve for three years and may be re-elected. In addition to carrying out the policies of the Assembly and serving as its adviser, the Board is given authority to take emergency measures within the financial capacity of the Organization in case of epidemics and calamities.

THE SECRETARIAT

The Secretariat comprises the Director-General and whatever technical and administrative staff may be required. In addition to his duties as chief technical and administrative officer, the Director-General appoints members of committees chosen from panels of experts who advise WHO on technical and scientific matters.

Activities

The activities of WHO fall into two main groups: advisory services and technical services. The work being carried on by the malaria control team of which Mrs. Bille-Brahe was a member is a good example of WHO advisory service. What this team was doing was applying the "know-how" that had been gained in other parts of the world to a specific problem in India. Such an exchange of knowledges and techniques among world neighborhoods has produced dramatic results. Active malaria cases in Greece dropped from 2,000,000 in 1942 to 50,000 in 1950. In the Philippines school absences were cut from 40 per cent in 1946 to 3 per cent in 1949 after malaria-control demonstrations were held. In South Africa malaria control increased the land under production from 700 acres to 12,000 acres in ten years. It is WHO's job to gather information on successful experiences throughout the world and transfer them to other regions when requested by governments to do so.

Demonstration teams or individual consultants carry on their work in a wide variety of fields, including tuberculosis, maternal and child care, nutrition, and sanitation. In addition, WHO coordinates a rapidly expanding fellowship program under which citizens of one country may study in another, gaining experience they may later apply at home.

WHO's technical services include the developing of international standards for vaccines and drugs. Another important service keeps the world informed of epidemics such as cholera and smallpox. Facts and figures on epidemics are broadcast throughout the world by radio transmitters. Plagues have been kept from spreading because WHO served as an organization through which many governments could help the peoples of a stricken area. WHO carries on special research projects on diseases such as influenza and poliomyelitis. In addition, WHO issues technical bulletins and publications that are used by medical scientists and public health officials throughout the world.

It is important to understand that the World Health Organization is *not* a "world sickness organization." No organization within itself could ever dare hope to administer to the health needs of the two billion people on earth. Nor is this the purpose of WHO. WHO is a workshop dedicated to helping the neighborhoods of the world help themselves, not only toward the eradication of disease but to "a state of complete physical, mental and social well-being" without which international good will cannot flourish.

THE UNITED NATIONS CHILDREN'S FUND: UNICEF

Headquarters: United Nations, New York, N. Y.

Origin

UNICEF is *not* a Specialized Agency of the United Nations. The United Nations International Children's Emergency Fund was created by unanimous vote of the United Nations General Assembly on December 11, 1946. On that date UNICEF became an integral part of the United Nations.

Purpose

UNICEF was established for the purpose of bringing assistance to children of war-devastated countries and raising the level of child health conditions. In December 1950 the General Assembly directed UNICEF to shift its emphasis from emergency relief to aid for long-range child care programs, particularly in underdeveloped countries. Emergency aid is also given children suffering from catastrophes such as earthquakes and floods, as well as those suffering from the dislocations of war.

To accomplish its purpose UNICEF, within its financial limitations, provides governments with the equipment they need to start mass nutrition and anti-disease campaigns for their children and to carry them on permanently with local people and local facilities after UNICEF aid ceases. Each dollar that UNICEF contributes to a program *must be matched by at least* an equal amount by the government receiving assistance. This policy underscores UNICEF's belief that the primary responsibility for the care of children is that of the individual country concerned.

Structure and Organization

UNICEF is governed by an Executive Board of twenty-six members. Eighteen of these are the members of the Social Commission of the Economic and Social Council of the United Nations. The other eight members are chosen by the Economic and Social Council. The Executive Board meets at least twice a year for the purpose of deciding upon allocations for UNICEF programs and to review progress and policies. The Executive Board is responsible to the Economic and Social Council, which in turn is responsible to the General Assembly of the United Nations.

The policies of the Executive Board are carried out by the Executive Director, who is appointed by the Secretary-General of the United Nations. The Executive Director has a staff of approximately 130, all of whom are members of the United Nations Secretariat.

Activities

We have seen how Mrs. Bille-Brahe and the malaria-control team were dependent upon UNICEF for DDT, maternity kits for midwives, and powdered milk. This is but one of thousands of ongoing UNICEF activities.

In seven years UNICEF has reached 60,000,000 children (one out of every fifteen in the world) with some form of aid. UNICEF has helped vaccinate 20,000,000 against TB, and has provided

e of the 22 spraying squads
rking with the WHO-UNICEF
m in the jungle villages of
ssa State (India) weighing out
T powder before spraying the
age. Each bag of powder will
mixed with two gallons of water
make one filling for the sprayer.

Workers spray DDT for mosquito
control in a village of the Terai
region in the foothills of the Hima-
layas.

School children doing "twig toothbrush" drill under the supervision
of the WHO-UNICEF Malaria
Control Team nurse and her local
assistant. Twigs and powdered
charcoal dentrifice are within the
means of all.

School children in a Malnad village
(Mysore State, India) go through
"personal hygiene" drill under the
supervision of WHO-UNICEF
Public Health Nurses.

The Universal Postal Union stamp design was chosen by an international jury of five experts appointed by the Secretary-General of the United Nations.

The "Refugee" stamp shown here was issued by the United Nations Postal Administration on 24 April 1953 to remind the world that the rehabilitation of refugees is a continuing

This stamp, a commemorative of the signing of the UN Charter in San Francisco on 26 June 1945, was issued on UN Day, 1952, Oct. 24 at UN Headquarters in New York.

A commemorative stamp for Human Rights Day was issued on 10 December 1952.

For the convenience of philatelists and visitors to the United Nations Headquarters, stamps

On 24 October 1951 the United Nations issued the first international postage stamps.

This 5-cent stamp is dedicated to the United Nations Children's Fund.

eighteen countries with equipment with which they produce vaccine locally and hence control TB on a continuing basis. UNICEF milk is fed to an average of 4,000,000 children a *day*, and twenty countries have been provided with pasteurizing and powdering equipment sufficient to produce safe milk for 5,000,000 more. Fifteen million children have been protected against malaria.

On the UNICEF story goes: training for midwives in Thailand, Pakistan, and Brazil; child-welfare clinics in the Philippines and Burma, and two thousand more throughout Asia and Latin America; milk and other foods for school lunches in Austria, Japan, and Guatemala; BCG to fight tuberculosis, DDT to fight the insect-borne diseases, penicillin to fight the disfigurement of yaws; research centers in Paris and Calcutta.

All of this and more, without bombast, without table thumping, without debate. Just thousands of Mrs. Bille-Brahes wending their ways along the trails that link the neighborhoods of the underdeveloped areas of the world, bringing with them a better now and a brighter future, leaving behind them trained people to carry on their work and a new meaning to "the brotherhood of man."

Finances

UNICEF is supported entirely by the *voluntary* contributions of the peoples and governments of one hundred countries. In six years UNICEF has distributed $180,000,000 to programs in eighty-one countries—an amount that has been at least matched by all the receiving countries.

Because contributions to UNICEF are voluntary, it is extremely difficult to do a thoroughgoing job of long-range planning. UNICEF set a projects allocation goal of $20,000,000 in 1952, but received $4,354,000 less than this amount. The projects goal for 1953 was established again at $20,000,000 to be allocated, if contributed, as follows:

Africa	$1,860,000
Asia	5,630,000
Eastern Mediterranean	1,850,000
Europe	600,000
Latin America	2,460,000
Programs benefiting more than one region	500,000
Emergency Situations	2,870,000
Freight	2,000,000
Administration and Operational Services	2,230,000
	$20,000,000

In March 1953 the Executive Board approved an allocation of $5,300,000 in new aid projects for forty-six countries. This reduced the UNICEF resources to $2,600, and further expenditures for that year depended upon the receipt of pledges and new contributions.

Government contributions to UNICEF increased in number and amount in 1953, as they have for the past several years. As of December 15, 47 governments, including the Vatican State, had contributed or pledged $13,900,000 to UNICEF for 1953. In 1952, 39 governments contributed $10,781,000.

Although governments have contributed the great bulk of funds to UNICEF, the organization's files attest to the fact that UNICEF purpose and spirit have reached people everywhere. A ninety-two-year-old woman of Mrs. Bille-Brahe's home town of Copenhagen, Denmark, contributed 1,000 crowns ($145) of her hard-earned savings from working days with the message: "I give this money to UNICEF where it will help a little child." At Christmas 1952, thirty staff members of the Arthur Godfrey radio-television program collected $1,668 for UNICEF instead of buying one another presents. In 499 communities youngsters turned the traditional "Trick or Treat" of Hallowe'en into "Trick or Treat for UNICEF," and collected over $32,000. This amount would enable UNICEF to purchase enough DDT to protect 640,000 people against malaria! "Trick or Treat for UNICEF" also resulted in the smallest gift ever received by the organization: three pennies, wrapped in an old handkerchief, addressed "To the World's Children" from "Jimmy."

The Future

The delegates to the Eighth Session of the General Assembly that met in New York in the Fall of 1953 voted unanimously to continue UNICEF on a permanent basis. For purposes of official record the organization will be known as the United Nations Children's Fund. But because the abbreviation "UNICEF" has become a symbol for humanity and brotherhood throughout the world, its use will be continued.

POSTMARKED "UNITED NATIONS, NEW YORK"

Universal Postal Union

On OCTOBER 24, 1951, the United Nations issued *international* postage stamps. For the first time in history an organization of nations produced stamps for world-wide circulation. This date marked an important milestone in international cooperation as well as in philately. The first day of issue was an appropriate commemoration of the UN's fifth year of dedication to world peace.

These new international symbols had their origin on November 16, 1950, when the General Assembly unanimously adopted a resolution establishing the United Nations Postal Administration and authorizing it to issue United Nations postage stamps. With this authority the Secretary-General of the United Nations began negotiations with the government of the United States which led to the special United Nations-United States Postal Agreement that was signed March 28, 1951.

Under the provisions of this agreement the United Nations was to issue and use its own postage stamps. A United Nations post office station was to be opened on the date of issue of UN stamps, with services and personnel provided by the United States Post Office Department. All mail postmarked "United Nations, New York" was to be stamped with United Nations stamps furnished to the U. S. Post Office without charge. United Nations postage stamps were to be valid only for postal purposes in the United Nations Headquarters' post office.

By the beginning of 1954 over fifteen million stamps had been issued through the United Nations Postal Administration. Of this number, well over half were used on nine million pieces of mail processed through the United Nations post office, and the remainder had been purchased by stamp collectors throughout the world. Proceeds from sales to collectors have proved a valuable source of income to the United Nations. The Secretary-General in his report to the General Assembly in November 1952 indicated that the United Nations Postal Administration had in a fifteen-month period a net profit of $474,524.52.

Far more important than monetary profit is the fact that the United Nations postage stamps have carried word of the Organization to the far corners of the globe. The stamps are designed to show the aims, work, and activities of the United Nations and its related organizations. The organization that makes it possible for these messages of peace, justice, and security to be transmitted to the neighborhoods of the world is the Universal Postal Union (UPU), a Specialized Agency of the United Nations.

The Universal Postal Union has more members than any other of the Specialized Agencies. It includes the postal administrations of eighty-two nations and eleven territories. UPU's basic principle is that, for postal purposes, all member states form a single territory. A partial glimpse of UPU's many activities may be had by following a letter postmarked "United Nations, New York" and addressed to Moscow, U.S.S.R.

The purchase price of a stamp for a letter weighing an ounce or less from the United States to the Soviet Union is eight cents. This same postage rate applies to all letters destined to most postal services throughout the world, thus underscoring the UPU's successful drive toward a single postal territory. Exceptions to this letter rate apply to mail intended for delivery by the postal services of member nations in the Postal Union of the Americas and Spain.

All of the American republics, Canada, and Spain are members of this Union. Agreements among these nations provide that the domestic rate will be charged for regular mail exchanged among member nations. Currently the rate from the United States to these countries is three cents—subject to change should the Congress pass, and the President approve, a law to raise the postage rates. Such regional organizations are authorized by the provisions of the Universal Postal Union Conventions.

A customer might purchase any one of the United Nations eight-cent postage stamps for this letter. As has been noted, these stamps are furnished free of charge to the United Nations post office. The money received from the sale of this stamp is retained by the United States Post Office Department. The members of UPU have agreed that each country is to keep all of the postage it collects. Prior to this decision a state of chaos existed, since postage collections for international mail were shared by the various postal administrations through which the mail passed in proportion to the services each country was supposed to have rendered. This division of postage money made for a very elaborate and costly system of accounting in each post office. While some senders might have enjoyed the game of determining what was the least costly route over which their mail might be sent, in the main there was intolerable confusion in the international postal service. Now, under UPU, each country keeps the postage it collects, and settles with other countries for their services on the basis of *weight* rather than *rates*.

Mail from the United Nations post office is taken by truck to the main post office in New York City. Here the postal officials whose responsibility it is to dispatch international mail have access to dozens of services provided by UPU agreements. While the processing of a letter directed to Moscow is a routine matter for these experienced people, there are times when UPU publications must be consulted. The International Bureau of the UPU provides member nations with such information as: complete information on the air-mail services of all UPU members, including a list of airports, showing ownership and geographical location; maps showing the routes of some six hundred airlines; a directory of post offices throughout the world; statements of rates; lists of prohibited articles; regulations governing the classification of mail into such categories as letters, commercial papers, post cards, samples and the like; a world map of surface communication routes, including railway, road, river, and sea facilities, capitals, frontier offices of exchange, ports, and postal centers.

Based upon this latter information, the port of destination is determined; in this case Hamburg, Germany. The mail for Moscow is kept open until shortly before ship departure time and then is placed in United States Mail pouches, weighed, and labeled. The ship upon which this letter will be forwarded is designated by United States postal officials, and poundage rates are paid the shipping company as provided by United States Postal Laws and Regulations.

Upon arrival at Hamburg, one of the most important of UPU's principles becomes operative. This is that every country is obliged to let foreign mail matter circulate within its territory on the same basis as its own, and for a just and reasonable compensation to forward it to its destination by the most rapid means available under its classification. This principle applies as the pouch is forwarded by rail to Berlin, through Warsaw and Brest in Poland, and across the border of the U.S.S.R. to Moscow.

The mail is received at the Central Telephone and Telegraph Building in Moscow. Article 151 of the UPU Regulations of Execution of the Convention of Paris provides that the United States Mail pouch shall be returned empty, by the next mail, to this country. Other UPU regulations affect the delivery of mail; articles addressed to persons who have submitted change of address are to be forwarded, unless the letter bears instructions to the contrary in the language of the country of destination, after delivery has been unsuccessfully attempted; the special-delivery indication on special-delivery articles may be stricken out; and many others.

By much the same procedure, mail from Moscow reaches the United States. The postage rate for a letter mailed from Moscow to St. Louis is 40 kopecks, a sum equal to about nine cents in United States currency. The mail usually follows the return mail route through to Berlin, and is then either forwarded to Cherbourg and Havre, France, or to Hamburg. By UPU regulation the postal administration forwarding the mail determines the shipping lines to be used. Vessels of the Cunard, Holland-America, French, and United States lines are used. An occasional dispatch from Hamburg is conveyed by the Home Lines.

The United States government becomes responsible for such mail upon delivery of same to the United States Post Office by the conveying vessel. The average transit time for mails from Moscow to the United States is twelve to nineteen days, depending upon shipping schedules. In the first seven months of 1952 mails were received from the U.S.S.R. on twenty-one occasions.

The Universal Postal Union has designated its International Bureau as a clearing house for the settlement of accounts among member nations who may want to take advantage of this service. Although the United States Post Office Department settles all accounts direct with the postal authorities concerned, its figures attest to the magnitude of international mail service. In the year ending June 30, 1952, the United States paid $9,127,093.29 to other Administrations and received $10,485,682.10. Of this latter amount $139,695 was for accounts owed to U.S. flag steamship companies for the conveyance of mails of other countries, and $5,783,640 was for the account of United States air carriers for similar services by air.

Letter communication between the neighborhoods of the world

has become such a simple, everyday affair that most of us take it for granted. But behind the modern efficiency of letter post are centuries of struggle on the part of the human community. No more vital contribution than that of the Universal Postal Union exists in postal history. Today the members of the UPU handle over 60,000,000,000 letters a year. The UPU purpose has never been more clearly defined than in the words of Mr. Gunner F. E. Lager, formerly Assistant Director of Posts in Sweden and Dean of the Thirteenth Universal Postal Congress held in Brussels, Belgium, in 1952. He addressed its opening session as follows:

> The purpose of our Union is clearly defined: organize and improve the postal service. Its only concern is to facilitate spiritual and material intercourse between men and nations. In that task, it takes no account of geographical frontiers, nor of barriers erected by differences in ideology, race or religion. In its province, it has made true that ancient dream which is always alive in the minds of men of good will: make the World one.

UNIVERSAL POSTAL UNION: UPU

International Headquarters:
Schwartorstrasse 38, Berne, Switzerland

Origin

The suggestion for the establishment of an international organization to handle postal matters originated in the United States. In 1862 Mr. Montgomery Blair, then Postmaster General of the United States, communicated with postal officials throughout the world urging that an international postal conference be held for the purpose of exchanging ideas that might bring some order out of the chaos then existing in the international postal service. It is interesting to note that Postmaster General Blair's suggestion was made at a time when his own country was engaged in the great internal struggle of the Civil War.

In 1863 the representatives of fifteen nations met at Paris for the first international postal conference. They adopted thirty-one articles of "general principles of such a nature as to facilitate relations among peoples, through the postal service, capable of being used as a basis for international conventions governing such relations." While no international organization was created at this meeting, the possibility of doing so at a future date was discussed by the delegates.

At the suggestion of Heinrich von Stephan, then Director-General of Posts of the North German Confederation, the first Postal Congress met at Berne, Switzerland, in 1874. After deliberating less than a month the delegates signed a "Treaty Concerning the Creation of a General Postal Union," subject to the ratification of their governments. This latter was accomplished on May 3, 1875, and brought about great and constructive changes in the international postal services.

The second Postal Congress, held at Paris in 1878, changed the name of the General Postal Union to the Universal Postal Union. The Twelfth Congress of the Universal Postal Union met at Paris in 1947, and adopted a proposition that established the UPU as a Specialized Agency of the United Nations. The Thirteenth Universal Postal Congress met at Brussels in May 1952.

Purpose

Article I of the Universal Postal Convention says the aim of the Universal Postal Union "is to secure the organization and improvement of the various international postal services, and to promote the development of international collaboration in this sphere." To attain this goal the countries which concluded the Convention form a single postal territory for the reciprocal exchange of correspondence.

Functions

All members of the UPU agree to follow the provisions of the Convention regulating the transmission of eight types of letter post: letters, single and reply-paid post cards, commercial papers, printed matter, raised print for the blind, samples of merchandise, small packets, and phonopost articles (such as phonograph records). Further provisions fix international maximum and minimum rates, weight limits, and dimensions for this type of mail. Under the provisions of Article II of the Final Protocol of the Convention, each country can increase the basic rates laid down in the Convention by 40 per cent as a maximum, or reduce them by 20 per cent as a maximum.

By agreements supplementing the Convention, and binding only for those members that adhere to them, the UPU regulates certain other postal services: insured letters and boxes, parcel post, money orders, postal transfers, collection orders, subscriptions to newspapers and periodicals, and cash-on-delivery articles.

Membership

As has been noted, the UPU with ninety-three members is the largest of the Specialized Agencies. A complete list of members appears in the Appendix.

The Universal Postal Union is an organization without any political ramifications whatever. Its work is purely administrative and technical.

Structure and Organization

The Universal Postal Union is composed of the Universal Postal Congress, the Executive and Liaison Committee, and the International Bureau of the UPU.

THE UNIVERSAL POSTAL CONGRESS

The Universal Postal Congress, or legislative body, is composed of representatives of all members of the Union. It usually meets every five years to review the Convention and its subsidiary agreements on the basis of proposals submitted by the members.

THE EXECUTIVE AND LIAISON COMMITTEE

The Permanent Executive and Liaison Committee consists of nineteen members elected on a geographical basis by each Congress. The Committee normally meets once a year in Berne. Its functions include the maintenance of relations with member nations, the study of technical questions relating to the international postal service, and the establishment and maintenance of working relations with the United Nations and other international organizations. The Committee also controls the activities of the International Bureau and on the recommendation of the Swiss government appoints its Director.

THE INTERNATIONAL BUREAU

The International Bureau is the administrative organ of the UPU. It assembles, coordinates, publishes, and distributes information of all kinds essential to the various postal administrations. The Bureau serves postal administrations as a clearing house for accounts if they so request. The Bureau makes preparations for Congresses and performs other functions assigned to it by the Convention.

Activities

In addition to the activities mentioned previously, the UPU provides other services to its members through the International Bureau. These include the distribution to other members of stamps of all types used by each member, supplying members with international reply coupons to cover the cost of return postage, exchanging information on postal equipment, and the exchange of films on postal subjects.

5

ILO

BOATMEN ON THE RHINE

International Labor Organization

THE RHINE RIVER has from early times been one
of the chief waterways of Europe. Rising in Switzerland, the Rhine
flows in a northerly direction, touching upon neighborhoods in the
German Federal Republic, France, and the Netherlands, and is
linked by canals to Belgium. These neighborhoods are rich in mineral
resources and produce goods that are shipped to all parts of the
world from the great ports of Rotterdam, Antwerp, and Amsterdam.

Nearly eight thousand freighters, passenger boats, tugs and
lighters constantly ply the 550 navigable miles of the Rhine, providing
trading facilities essential to the economic life of the regions they
serve. Forty-five thousand people, the Rhine boatmen and their
families, live and work on the river. The average barge carries a crew
of two or three in addition to the skipper and his family.

Life is both hazardous and hard for the Rhine boatmen.
Handling heavy bulk cargoes such as fuel, coal, sugar, and cereals
is a difficult task. Routine chores aboard ship, such as painting,
cleaning the smokestacks, and maintaining steam engines, have their
dangerous moments. The hours are long. For the crew members this
is a lonely life, since it may mean being away from home for weeks
at a time.

While the work to be done does not vary much from one craft
to another, the same cannot be said for labor conditions. The river
boats are owned by individuals and companies of five different

nations. This means that there are five different standards of employment regarding wages, hours of work, vacations, and the like.

Until June of 1953 the same confusion and hardship existed in medical care and social security protection. Before this date, if a Rhine boatman became ill or was injured, he did not qualify for free medical care or accident allowance under the social security laws of his own or other countries. Too, the Rhine boatman found it difficult to qualify for a pension after his working days were over, as there was no system for coordinating retirement payments.

The story of how the Rhine boatmen came to have social security protection without regard to national boundaries is a story of cooperation and good will by owners, unions, and governments working through the International Labor Organization (ILO), a Specialized Agency of the United Nations.

Labor problems resulting from situations where more than one nation used a common waterway had long been the concern of ILO. As early as 1920 the Organization had recommended that owners, workers, and governments sharing common waterways should standardize on an eight-hour day and a forty-eight-hour week. Prior to the outbreak of World War II, the International Labor Organization had made many studies regarding particular problems connected with inland transport of all types. Following the war, ILO established an Inland Transport Committee as a permanent group charged with the responsibility for furthering ILO's purposes by bringing together employer, worker, and government representatives who were experts in this field. This Committee recognized the special problems of the boatmen on the Rhine and on the canals of the Rhine basin.

Many of the owners of Rhine craft were aware of the inequalities of the special security protection afforded their employees. In February of 1947 the Committee of French Owners of Rhine Shipping adopted a resolution suggesting that a social insurance system for workers in Rhine navigation should be dealt with in an international convention between governments represented on the Central Commission for Rhine Navigation. This latter organization was set up under the provisions of the Congress of Vienna in 1815. Although modified by subsequent treaties, the major purpose of the Commission has remained the same since that date—to insure that the navigation of the Rhine and its mouths shall be free to vessels and people of all nations for the transportation of goods and persons.

It remained for Rhine boatmen to take the initiative in this matter. Through their union they appealed to the International Transportworkers' Federation with which they were affiliated, and which represents some 5,500,000 workers in over forty different countries. The ITF decided to convene a Rhine Navigation Conference to discuss working conditions in Rhine shipping. This Conference, held in 1946, adopted a provisional program for conditions of employment for the Rhine boatmen. It also authorized a committee to approach the International Labor Organization with a view to promoting agreements on social insurance for Rhine navigation workers.

The International Transportworkers' Federation subsequently stated the case for the Rhine boatmen in a letter sent to the Director-General of ILO at Geneva, Switzerland, on March 14, 1947, and signed by the General-Secretary of the ITF, Mr. J. H. Oldenbroek. This letter advised the Director-General that ITF planned to raise these matters in behalf of the Rhine boatmen at the next meeting of the Inland Transport Committee of the ILO. The ITF suggested that since any agreements would involve German workers, it would be advisable to invite representatives from the United States and the United Kingdom, two of the three powers then occupying Western Germany; the third was France, a country directly concerned in its own right.

Mr. Oldenbroek's letter stated a particular case for social security. He noted that workers living in one country forfeit their social security claims in that country when working on a vessel of another nationality. The ITF suggested as a basis for discussion at the Inland Transport Committee meeting that for medical aid and sickness benefits the boatman should be treated as a national of the country for which he was working, but for incapacity or retirement, as a national of his own country. With this letter the ITF submitted a list of minimum claims of the Rhine shipping workers as to hours of work, rest periods, minimum wages, overtime, and annual vacations, plus some other items.

The Director-General of ILO circulated the communication from the ITF among the government, employer, and worker delegates to the Inland Transport Committee, as well as to its general membership. This gave the delegates adequate time to prepare for discussion on this matter before the meeting of the Inland Transport Committee held at Geneva in May 1947. The ITC established a Subcommittee on Rhine Navigation, consisting of eighteen members representing Belgium, France, Netherlands, Switzerland, United Kingdom, and the United States, and balanced so that six members represented the governments, six the workers, and six the employers.

The Subcommittee on Rhine Navigation met at Geneva in May 1947. The members unanimously adopted a resolution that recognized the hardships that existed for the Rhine boatmen because of differences in laws and regulations as well as differences in collective agreements in the various countries, and recommended that the governments concerned should hold a special tripartite (government-employer-worker) conference to consider drafting conventions to correct conditions. The Subcommittee further charged the International Labor Organization to provide detailed reports and all documentation necessary for such a conference.

Acting upon this authority, the International Labor Office accomplished the background research. The Director-General of ILO handled the exchange of views of the governments concerned, and

Life is both hazardous and hard for the Rhine boatmen. Here an invalid boatman is shown working an anchor hoist.

ch Captain M. van Dam, owner of the e boat "God mit Uns," with his wife in r living quarters.

The wife of a seaman is shown hanging laundry on the deck of the "Richebourg."

The kitchen on board the "Richebourg."

The grocery boat supplies goods to the wife of a Rhine boatman in Duisburg harbor.

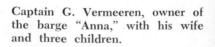

Captain G. Vermeeren, owner of the barge "Anna," with his wife and three children.

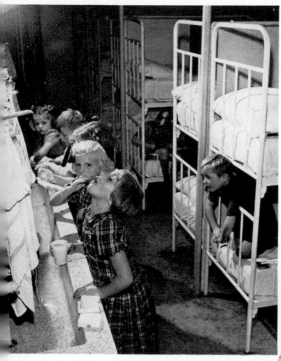

Boarding school for children of the Rhine boatmen on a remodelled barge in Rotterdam harbor.

Crew of a German steam tug in their quarters.

The German Federal Republic is represented by government, worker, and employer delegates to the ILO Conference on Rhine Boatmen held at Geneva, Switzerland on 31 October 1949. This was the first meeting of a Specialized Agency of the United Nations to which the government, whose capital is at Bonn, had sent a delegation.

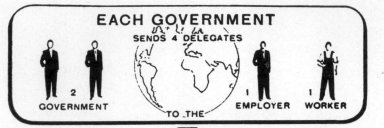

EACH GOVERNMENT

SENDS 4 DELEGATES

2
GOVERNMENT

TO THE

EMPLOYER 1   WORKER 1

INTERNATIONAL LABOUR CONFERENCE

WHICH EXAMINES SOCIAL PROBLEMS AND ADOPTS
CONVENTIONS AND RECOMMENDATIONS
FOR SUBMISSION TO GOVERNMENTS

THE CONFERENCE ELECTS THE

GOVERNING BODY

8 WORKERS

16 GOVERNMENTS

8 EMPLOYERS

WHICH SUPERVISES THE WORK OF THE

INTERNATIONAL LABOUR OFFICE

RESEARCH   INVESTIGATIONS   TECHNICAL ASSISTANCE   PUBLICATIONS

How the ILO works.

when all had signified their acceptance of the Subcommittee's resolution the ILO planned the Special Tripartite Conference concerning Rhine boatmen which opened at Geneva October 31, 1949. A delegation of the new German Federal Republic attended the Conference with representatives of the High Commissioners in Germany. This was the first meeting of a Specialized Agency of the United Nations to which the German Federal Republic had sent representatives. The International Labor Organization had been the first to admit a German delegation after World War I—the Washington Conference of 1919.

Basing its work upon drafts prepared by the International Labor Office, the Geneva Conference completed its work on December 14, 1949. After disagreements had been resolved harmoniously, the texts of two agreements were adopted unanimously. One concerned social security and the other dealt with working conditions. Under the draft agreement on social security, the insurance protection was to be granted by the country in which the head office of the employer was located. A boatman was to be insured for sickness and other benefits. If a boatman had social insurance benefits resulting from illness or injury outside the country that afforded his protection, the country in which his disability occurred was to provide the necessary services and was entitled to repayment by the insurance institution of the responsible country. Pension payments were to be made by each country in proportion to the time the boatman had been employed. The second agreement fixed minimum hours, holidays, and other working conditions. Some of the latter, such as limited time off to cover family responsibilities, were new in ILO history.

The draft agreements, with suggestions for their implementation, were submitted to the ILO Governing Body. After having approved the work of the Geneva Conference, the Governing Body convened a conference of government representatives at Paris in July 1950 for the purpose of approval in final form. This was accomplished with the further stipulation that the acceptances of the countries concerned were to be entrusted to the Director-General of ILO, who in turn would register them with the United Nations. The agreements were to become effective on the first day of the third month following deposit of ratification instruments by the governments of Switzerland, France, Belgium, the Federal Republic of Germany, and the Netherlands.

On March 4, 1953, Director-General David A. Morse of the International Labor Organization announced that the international convention on social security protection for the Rhine boatmen would become effective on June 1. This followed a brief ceremony at which Jean Leroy, permanent Belgian delegate to the ILO, deposited his country's ratification of the agreement. The conditions of employment agreement had at that time been ratified only by the German Federal Republic.

As the result of this international agreement the conditions of life and labor will be improved for the Rhine boatmen and their families. The ILO's contribution to the solution of this human problem was one of seeking an exchange of experiences upon which actions could be harmonized and international treaties written if the nations concerned so desired. By making it possible for governments, workers, and employers to resolve problems through democratic discussion and free decision, the ILO is contributing toward building a lasting peace.

INTERNATIONAL LABOR ORGANIZATION: ILO

International Headquarters: Geneva, Switzerland

Origin

The International Labor Organization was established on April 11, 1919, as an autonomous Organization associated with the League

of Nations. Samuel Gompers, who represented the United States
on the Commission on International Labor Legislation at the Versailles Peace Conference, and who was subsequently named Chairman of the Commission, was one of the leading advocates of this
international organization dedicated to improving living and working
conditions throughout the world. Although the United States did not
join ILO until 1934, the First International Labor Conference, held
at Washington, D.C., in October 1919 unanimously invited Gompers
to participate in its deliberations.

The twenty-sixth session of the General Conference of the International Labor Organization met at Philadelphia in 1944 and adopted
a Declaration of aims and purposes. This Declaration redefined the
original aims and purposes of ILO's Constitution which had formed
a part of the Treaty of Versailles and other treaties. Subsequent
sessions of the General Conference have amended the Constitution.

In 1946 the ILO became associated with the United Nations
as a Specialized Agency under the terms of an agreement which
recognized the responsibility of the ILO in the field of labor and
social conditions.

Purpose

The ILO purpose is stated in Article II of the Declaration of
Philadelphia.

> Believing that experience has fully demonstrated the truth
> of the Statement in the Constitution of the International
> Labour Organisation that lasting peace can be established
> only if it is based on social justice, the Conference affirms
> that:

> *a.* all human beings, irrespective of race, creed or sex, have
> the right to pursue both their material well-being and
> their spiritual development in conditions of freedom and
> dignity, of economic security and equal opportunity;

b. the attainment of the conditions in which this shall be possible must constitute the central aim of national and international policy;

c. all national and international policies and measures, in particular those of an economic and financial character, should be judged in this light and accepted only in so far as they may be held to promote and not to hinder the achievement of this fundamental objective;

d. it is a responsibility of the International Labour Organisation to examine and consider all international economic and financial policies and measures in the light of this fundamental objective;

e. in discharging the tasks entrusted to it the International Labour Organisation, having considered all relevant economic and financial factors, may include in its decisions and recommendations any provisions which it considers appropriate.

Functions

The ILO is charged with the following functions as established in Article III of the Declaration of Philadelphia:

The Conference recognises the solemn obligation of the International Labour Organisation to further among the nations of the world programs which will achieve:

a. full employment and the raising of standards of living;

b. the employment of workers in the occupations in which they can have the satisfaction of giving the fullest measure of their skill and attainments and make their greatest contribution to the common well-being;

c. the provision, as a means to the attainment of this end and under adequate guarantees for all concerned, of facilities for training and the transfer of labour, including migration for employment and settlement;

d. policies in regard to wages and earnings, hours and other conditions of work calculated to ensure a just share of the fruits of progress to all, and a minimum living wage to all employed and in need of such protection;

e. the effective recognition of the right of collective bargaining, the cooperation of management and labour in continuous improvement of productive efficiency, and the collaboration of workers and employers in the preparation and application of social and economic measures;

f. the extension of social security measures to provide a basic income to all in need of such protection and comprehensive medical care;

g. adequate protection for the life and health of workers in all occupations;

h. provision for child welfare and maternity protection;

i. the provision of adequate nutrition, housing and facilities for recreation and culture. . . .

Membership

As of May 1, 1954, ILO had sixty-seven members. A complete list of members is included in the Appendix.

Any member of the United Nations may become a member of ILO by accepting the obligations of membership. The admission of non-members of the UN must be approved by the General Conference.

Each nation assumes the responsibility of submitting Conventions approved by the ILO General Conference to its competent national authority to be considered for ratification. When a government ratifies a Convention, it submits annual reports to ILO on the steps taken to make the Convention effective.

Recommendations adopted by the ILO General Conference need not be submitted for ratification, but members are under obligation to consider giving effect to their provisions.

Members report periodically to ILO on the position of their law and practice regarding unratified Conventions and Recommendations.

Structure and Organization

The ILO has three principal organs: the General Conference, the Governing Body, and the International Labor Office.

THE GENERAL CONFERENCE

The General Conference is composed of two government delegates, one worker delegate, and one employer delegate from each member nation. The worker and employer delegates are chosen by the member nations after consultation with the most representative worker and employer organizations of the country.

The primary function of the General Conference is the formulation of international minimum standards of working and living conditions. A two-thirds vote of the delegates present is necessary to adopt these standards, which then become Conventions or Recommendations. Collectively these are known as the International Labor Code. ILO agreements become operative only in those member countries whose governments ratify them.

Other responsibilities charged to the General Conference at its annual sessions include: electing members of the Governing Body, adoption of the annual budget, and the review of reports from member states regarding the implementation of Conventions and Recommendations.

THE GOVERNING BODY

The Governing Body is composed of the representatives of sixteen governments, eight workers, and eight employers. Eight of the government seats are allocated to the countries of greatest industrial importance, and the other eight filled by election.

The Governing Body acts as the executive organ for ILO. It supervises various committees and commissions, drafts proposals for the budget, appoints the Director-General, and supervises the work of the International Labor Office.

INTERNATIONAL LABOR OFFICE

The International Labor Office is the permanent secretariat of the ILO. Its responsibilities include the following: preparing documents for ILO meetings; publishing periodicals, studies, and reports on social and economic matters; giving advice and assistance to governments, worker, and employer groups when requested to do so; providing machinery for making the Conventions effective.

The Director-General is responsible for the functioning of the International Labor Office.

SUPPLEMENTARY COMMITTEES, COMMISSIONS, AND CONFERENCES

Numerous committees, commissions, and conferences are essential to carrying out ILO's purposes. The Inland Transport Committee that created the Subcommittee on Rhine Navigation, and the Special Tripartite Conference that formally considered recommendations concerning the Rhine boatmen, are examples of such supplementary organizations.

Activities

The ILO employs a wide variety of methods in seeking to fulfill its purposes. The way in which its machinery may be utilized to solve problems brought to its attention by member governments, workers, and employers has been described in the case of the Rhine boatmen. A brief résumé of some projects sponsored by ILO under the 1953 expanded technical assistance program of the United Nations gives further evidence of the widespread activities of the Organization.

In Pakistan two ILO experts set up a demonstration vocational training center at Karachi. In Ceylon centers have been established for teaching carpentry and cotton spinning. An agreement signed between ILO and the government of Yugoslavia sent forty-four instructors into that country and provided training in foreign plants for more than 300 workers, specialists, and technicians.

ILO projects have led to the improvement of production techniques by the use of better methods and tools in Burma, Colombia, Egypt, Haiti, India, Syria, Thailand, and Turkey. Social security projects are under way in Bolivia, Cuba, Guatemala, Indonesia, Iraq, and Israel. Migration and employment service projects sponsored by ILO are helping the governments of Mexico and Uruguay solve problems in these areas. Industrial safety and industrial hygiene programs are more effective in Indonesia and Lebanon because of ILO technical assistance. Numerous surveys of labor statistics, manpower, industrial relations, industrial welfare, and inspection are being undertaken by ILO at the request of governments throughout the world.

Thus, by making it possible for governments, workers, and employers to improve working and living conditions, the International Labor Organization is helping to provide a firm basis upon which to build universal peace.

6

ITU

"NEW YORK CALLING DJAKARTA"

International Telecommunication Union

FROM EARLIEST TIMES neighborhoods of the world have had systems of distance communication. For thousands of years primitive man transmitted his messages by smoke signals, drums, and fire towers. Later the development of written languages enabled peoples to communicate through messages carried by pigeons and by riders on horseback. The Romans developed this latter system into a highly efficient postal service operating over the imperial roads. Caesar's letters written to Cicero from Britain were delivered in Rome within twenty-six days.

For many centuries there was no improvement over the Roman post that Caesar used in the first century B.C. A message transmitted from London to Rome in 1800 was seldom delivered within thirty days! But in the early years of this same century discoveries were being made that revolutionized communications over long distances. Pioneers such as Samuel F. B. Morse in the United States brought together knowledges that led to the development of the electromagnetic telegraph. In the 1840's Morse was granted $30,000 by Congress to construct an experimental telegraph line between Baltimore and Washington. In that same decade countries in Europe were being linked with signals transmitted by wire.

Side by side with improvements in overland telegraphy came inventions that made submarine telegraphy possible. In 1851 a cable was laid between Dover, England and Calais, France. Within the next few years other submarine cables were laid from England to other shores, between Denmark and Sweden, and between various points in the Mediterranean Sea. After two unsuccessful attempts a cable was laid under the Atlantic Ocean in 1866 that linked Valentia, Ireland, with Heart's Content, Newfoundland. In 1882 cable contact was established between the United States and countries in Central and South America. In 1906 the first and only trans-Pacific cable was laid. This linked the United States with Shanghai by way of Hawaii, Midway Island, Guam, and the Philippines. With these developments it became possible to flash signals between the neighborhoods of the world in a matter of minutes.

Other inventions, dating from those of Guglielmo Marconi in the 1890's, soon made it practicable to send telegraphy messages by radio. The first transocean radiotelegraph service was established in 1912 between San Francisco and Honolulu. This was followed in 1920 by the opening of a direct service from the United States to England. Services of this kind were gradually expanded until now it is possible for a person to send a radiotelegram to almost any place in the world.

During the latter part of the nineteenth century events were taking place that led to more intimate communication among peoples. On March 10, 1876, Alexander Graham Bell transmitted the first complete sentence heard over a wire, and the telephone became a reality. Beginning in 1877 with the first regular telephone line between Boston and Somerville, Massachusetts, service was gradually expanded until today a telephone subscriber in New York can be connected with 48,100,000 telephones in the United States.

After Marconi had successfully accomplished the transmission of telegraph signals by radio, other inventors began experimenting with telephone transmission by the same means. In 1915 speech was successfully transmitted from Arlington, Virginia, to Paris. On January 7, 1927, New York and London were first connected for commercial telephone service through the facilities of the Bell System. This service extended to other countries, and on April 25, 1935, the first 'round-the-world telephone circuit was established over a combination of radio and land line facilities. By 1953 it was possible for any subscriber in the domestic telephone system to be connected with 80,900,000 telephones outside the continental limits of the United States.

Typical of such a call is one between New York City and Djakarta, Indonesia. Most of the calls made between these two points are placed from New York between the hours of 9:30 A.M. to 10:30 A.M. and between 6:30 P.M. and 9:00 P.M. Because of the time differential these calls are received at Djakarta between 10:00 P.M. and 11:00 P.M. the same day and between 7:00 A.M. and 9:30 A.M. the following day.

When the subscriber informs the long distance operator that he wants to place a call to Djakarta, she switches his call to the central overseas operating office. The overseas operator then makes the first attempt to complete the connection while the customer holds the line. The first contact the operator makes is by land wire or microwave relay to Oakland, California. At Oakland the call is relayed by radio transmitter across the Pacific Ocean to the Indonesian radio terminal station at Bandung. From this point the call goes by land wire to the central switchboard in Djakarta, where the operator uses the regular telephone system to reach the person for whom the call is intended. If there are no calls ahead of that placed by the customer, and if atmospheric difficulties do not interfere, the connection is completed in a matter of minutes.

While English is the language used by the operators handling this call, the customers may converse in the language of their choice. If at any time during the conversation the radiotelephone circuit is subject to static, noise, or fading, this time is compensated for by the operators so that the customer is guaranteed a clear connection.

The weekday rate for a three-minute message between New York and Djakarta is twelve dollars.

In settling accounts on this call the Bell System deals directly with the Indonesian Post, Telegraph and Telephone organization. Divisions of revenue are independent of the point of origin of the call. A moderate deduction is made by the Bell System because the land line service between New York and Oakland is longer than that between Bandung and Djakarta, and the remainder of the toll charge is divided between the two telephone systems.

Calls between New York and Djakarta are as important to the daily business of the world's neighborhoods as those we place through the local switchboard are to our own communities. The exporters use this service to speed the movement of the tobacco products, cotton goods, machinery, buses and trucks that we sell to the people of Indonesia. Importers utilize the overseas telephone service to regulate the flow of oil, rubber and hard fibers that we buy from the Indonesians. Government delegates to meetings at the United Nations are able to communicate with officials at Djakarta when matters of importance require decisions from the capital of Indonesia. The radiotelephone service is used for on-the-spot news broadcasts to keep the peoples of the world informed of international affairs. Communications over vast distances have become so commonplace that this service may be looked upon as an intercontinental speech path linking our neighborhood with all parts of the world.

The development of radiotelegraphy and radiotelephony has led to many other important developments in the field of communications. Ships and aircraft are linked to shore points and to one another through both these services. The importance of these services is well illustrated by an Associated Press report carried by the papers on the date this was being written:

A weak distress signal sputtered for more than two hours

today from the sea lane between Wake Island and Hawaii, raising hopes for the persons on board the transocean airliner.

The Navy shifted its massive air and surface search closer to the Hawaiian end of the Wake-Honolulu run. It estimated that the sender was 300 to 800 miles west of Honolulu.

The signal was so weak that ships and planes were unable to get an accurate bearing.

But the distress call was heard continuously for more than two hours starting at 3 P.M., the Navy said. The signal was on an international wave band reserved for distress calls.

The reserving of the international distress frequency at 500 kilocycles is illustrative of the work of the International Telecommunication Union (ITU), a Specialized Agency of the United Nations. As has already been noted in Chapter 2, twice each hour radio operators on ships and planes the world over turn for a period of three minutes to this frequency, reserved for their fellow men who may be in distress.

The recording of frequency assignments is a function of the International Frequency Registration Board (IFRB), an integral part of ITU. Signals sent from place to place by radio are carried on a radio wave. The number of waves that pass a fixed point in a second determines the frequency of a wave. No two messages transmitted from stations in the same general locality can use the same frequency without jamming each other. As these radio highways have become more crowded, nations have joined together through the ITU so that each nation can use a particular group of radio frequencies without fear of its messages being jammed by the radio services of its neighbors. The development of radar and television and their utilization of high-frequency waves have posed new problems for the IFRB.

As international telecommunication becomes of increasing importance to the industry, government trade, finance, and social affairs of neighborhoods throughout the world, the finding of a common basis for the orderly and efficient transmission of signals between them will require both technical ingenuity and mutual cooperation and good will. In the ITU the nations of the world will find a workshop devoted to helping them solve their common telecommunication problems.

INTERNATIONAL TELECOMMUNICATION UNION: ITU

International Headquarters:
Palais Wilson, Geneva, Switzerland

Origin

In 1838 electrical telegraphy came into use in Europe. In the years that followed, various European nations concluded agreements that standardized operations and the collection of telegraph rates. These earlier agreements were followed by regional covenants involving nations in both Eastern and Western Europe. In 1865 twenty countries ratified a treaty signed at Paris that created the International Telegraph Union. This treaty was amended in 1885 to include the first provisions for international telegraph service.

By 1906 radiotelegraphy had become so generally used that twenty-seven countries realized international agreements were necessary in this field. As a result these nations banded together to form the International Radiotelegraph Union at a convention signed in Berlin.

The International Telecommunication Union formally came into being on January 1, 1934. The ITU resulted from the merger of the International Telegraph Union and the International Radiotelegraph Union following a conference held in Madrid in 1932.

The International Telecommunication Convention was completely redrafted in 1947 by the Plenipotentiary and International Radio Conferences held at Atlantic City, New Jersey. By an agreement approved by the General Assembly of the United Nations in 1947 and annexed to the Atlantic City Convention, the ITU in its new form became a Specialized Agency related to the United Nations.

Purposes

The purposes of the International Telecommunication Union are established in the Atlantic City Convention as follows:

a. to maintain and extend international cooperation for the improvement and rational use of telecommunication of all kinds;

b. to promote the development of technical facilities and their most efficient operation with a view to improving the efficiency of telecommunication services, increasing their usefulness and making them, so far as possible, generally available to the public;

c. to harmonize the actions of nations in the attainment of those common ends.

Functions

To accomplish these purposes the Atlantic City Convention charges ITU with these particular functions:

a. effect allocation of the radio frequency spectrum and registration of radio frequency assignments in order to avoid harmful interference between radio stations of different countries;

b. foster collaboration among its Members and Associate Members with a view to the establishment of rates at

levels as low as possible consistent with an efficient
service and taking into account the necessity for maintaining independent financial administration of telecommunication on a sound basis;

c. promote the adoption of measures for assuring the safety
of life through the cooperation of telecommunication services;

d. undertake studies, formulate recommendations, and collect
and publish information on telecommunication matters
for the benefit of all Members and Associate Members.

Membership

As of May 1, 1954, ITU had ninety members and four associate
members. This is the second largest membership among the Specialized Agencies, exceeded only by the Universal Postal Union. A complete list of members appears in the Appendix.

Non-members of the United Nations may become members of
ITU if their applications are approved by two-thirds of the members
of the Union. Each member has one vote at all ITU conferences and
meetings of ITU organizations of which it is a member. Any trust
territory or group of territories not entirely responsible for the conduct of their own international affairs, may be admitted as associate
members of ITU, without vote.

Structure and Organization

The structure of the ITU consists of a Plenipotentiary Conference, Administrative Conferences, and the permanent organs of the
Union: the Administrative Council, the General Secretariat, the International Frequency Registration Board, the International Telegraph Consultative Committee, the International Telephone Consultative Committee, and the International Radio Consultative Committee.

The overseas switchboard marked "Via Oakland" where calls originating in New York City for Djakarta are routed to the overseas operator in Oakland, California.

e overseas switchboard in Oakland, lifornia where calls are handled between New York City and Djakarta.

exterior view of the radio station at Dixon, lifornia which transmits telephone calls to donesia as well as to Hawaii, Australia, New aland, Guam, the Philippine Islands, Okiwa, China, Korea, and Hong Kong.

The overseas control terminal in Oakland, California where a technical operator maintains the radiotelephone circuit on calls to Djakarta.

Indonesian overseas operators receive calls from New York at the radio terminal station in Bandung.

From Bandung the call goes by land wire to the central switchboard in Djakarta.

An operator in Djakarta uses the regular telephone system to reach the person for whom the call is intended. This connection is completed a few minutes after the customer in New York originates the call.

View of the Palais Wilson in Geneva, Switzerland, Headquarters of the International Telecommunication Union.

PLENIPOTENTIARY CONFERENCE

The Plenipotentiary Conference is the supreme organ of the ITU. All members of the Union are members of the Conference, which normally meets once every five years. The most recent meeting of the Conference was held in Buenos Aires in 1952. It considers the reports of the Administrative Council; establishes the basis of the ITU budget for a five-year period; elects members of the Administrative Council; revises the ITU Convention when necessary; enters into formal agreements with other international bodies; and deals with whatever telecommunications questions are presented. Other than decisions relating to the admission of new members, all action is by majority vote.

ADMINISTRATIVE CONFERENCES

All members of the ITU may be represented at Administrative Conferences. The Administrative Telegraph and Telephone Conference and the Administrative Radio Conference revise the Administrative Regulations in these fields. Although Administrative Conferences generally meet at the same time and place as the Plenipotentiary Conference, special sessions may be convened if twenty nations so indicate their desire, or upon proposal of the Administrative Council.

ADMINISTRATIVE COUNCIL

The Administrative Council is composed of eighteen members elected by the Plenipotentiary Conference. The Council supervises ITU administrative affairs between meetings of the Plenipotentiary Conference, reviews and approves the annual budget, appoints the Secretary-General and the two Assistant Secretaries-General, and coordinates the work of the Union with other international organizations. The Council normally meets once a year, but can be convened in special session at the request of six members.

GENERAL SECRETARIAT

Under the direction of the Secretary-General of ITU the General Secretariat carries out the administrative work of the Union. It carries out the work preparatory to and following meetings within the Union; it publishes recommendations and reports of the permanent organs of the Union; it issues other information of importance to the members, such as international or regional telecommunication agreements. The General Secretariat also prepares the annual budget for submission to the Administrative Council.

INTERNATIONAL FREQUENCY REGISTRATION BOARD

The IFRB consists of eleven members, appointed by as many members of the ITU elected on a regional basis by the Administrative Radio Conference. Members serve, not as members of their countries, or of a region, but "as custodians of an international public trust." The IFRB records all frequency assignments and furnishes advice to members of ITU with a view to the operation of the maximum number of radio channels.

CONSULTATIVE COMMITTEES

Three international consultative committees, one each for radio, telegraph, and telephone, have been created for the purpose of studying technical and operating questions in these fields and issuing recommendations to the respective Administrative Conferences.

Activities

Scientific and technological advances in the field of telecommunications, plus the ever-increasing use of these facilities throughout the world, have posed exacting and difficult problems for the ITU.

One ongoing activity has been the preparation of a new worldwide radio frequency allocation table. This undertaking began with a series of conferences between countries using maritime, aeronautical, and broadcasting facilities in the several regions of the world. At each conference plans were drawn up whereby each station, or group of stations, would be assigned one or more frequencies on which to carry out its transmission. The final draft plans would then be submitted to the approval of a final administrative conference to which all member nations would be invited. Then by orderly process it was hoped that a new frequency allocation table would be brought into operation which would harmonize radio facilities throughout the world.

The Cairo Conference of 1938 had provided for such a table, ranging from 10 kilocycles per second (kc/s) to 200,000 kc/s. The impact of scientific advance in this field can be best appreciated by the recommendation of the Atlantic City Radio Conference of 1947 that the new table extend from 10 kc/s to 10,500,000 kc/s! Add to this the understandable desire of nations and services to further their own effectiveness by utilizing the most effective channels, and one begins to realize the difficulties confronting ITU.

ITU provides many services without which international telecommunication would be impossible. It provides members with an international listing of telegraph offices and of radio frequencies. These become working documents in the offices of governmental and private companies, as well as in all kinds of stations: ship, aircraft, and land. Every two weeks ITU supplies current information on new or closed circuits, new rates and charges, and services temporarily suspended or reopened.

Technical studies and recommendations on such questions as television, protection of telephone lines, signaling and switching, letter and graphic symbols connected with telephony, tests and measurements of commercial telephone systems, and the like, are regular contributions made by ITU to its membership.

For nearly ninety years the International Telecommunication

Union has, link by link, sponsored a network of telecommunications among the neighborhoods of the world. The ITU has survived two world wars and has emerged from each a stronger instrument for world peace. No nation has ever withdrawn from this workshop for the world. No workshop has contributed more to the cause of internationalism.

Any subscriber in the domestic telephone system can be connected with 80,900,000 telephones outside the continental limits of the United States.

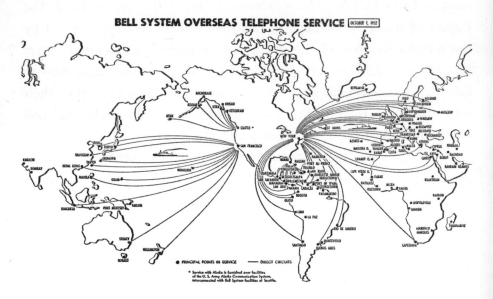

BELL SYSTEM OVERSEAS TELEPHONE SERVICE | OCTOBER 1, 1952 |

● PRINCIPAL POINTS IN SERVICE — DIRECT CIRCUITS

* Service with Alaska is furnished over facilities
of the U. S. Army Alaska Communication System,
interconnected with Bell System facilities at Seattle.

This Tarascan woman is drawing water from a well in one of the villages near the Patzcuaro Center.

A typical Tarascan school child.

A typical class of Tarascan children in a village school near Patzcuaro. These schools are the cultural centers of the Mexican villages where the Patzcuaro students usually plan and start their work.

Students in the Reading Room and Library at the Fundamental Education Center Headquarters. The script for a film strip is being studied.

When the film strip and lecture notes are completed the film strip is tested in the villages.

The day after the showing students follow up the program by hanging posters on the same subject around the village.

7
UNESCO

PUPILS AT PATZCUARO

United Nations Educational, Scientific and Cultural Organization

EACH WINTER members of boards of education in communities throughout the United States tackle the problem of their annual budgets. These boards are responsible for providing the best facilities for the education of their youth within the framework of state laws and the capacity and willingness of the citizens in their communities to pay for these facilities. These public-spirited citizens spend many long hours at the task of making ends meet—at the same time doing justice to students, teachers, and taxpayers. The amount of money they appropriate may be equal to several hundred dollars for each pupil enrolled in that particular school system.

The United Nations Educational, Scientific and Cultural Organization (UNESCO) is charged by its Constitution, among other responsibilities, to "give fresh impulse to popular education and to the spread of culture; by collaborating with Members, at their request, in the development of educational activities...." But among the UNESCO members in the Latin American community alone, millions of people can neither read nor write. If these people were to have the right to a free education—limited to elementary school only—the annual cost would exceed the budgets of the United Nations and all the Specialized Agencies combined! To extend such a basic education to the half of the world's population that is illiterate would involve a financial outlay staggering to the imagination.

When a group is confronted with a problem of this magnitude, there are two possible approaches. One is to regard the whole situation as hopeless—like trying to chop down a forest with a single ax —and to defer consideration of it indefinitely. Another is to realize that, while attempting to achieve universal education quickly would result only in frustration and failure, nevertheless techniques might be developed that would lead to a long-range accomplishment of the objectives. UNESCO wisely chose the latter course. For to ignore this universal tragedy would be to deny that the defenses of peace can be constructed in the minds of men.

The first step was to decide how UNESCO might go about developing these techniques. In 1946 a special committee to the Preparatory Commission of UNESCO published a document entitled *Fundamental Education, Common Ground for All Peoples.* Thirty-three international experts in the field of fundamental education contributed to this blueprint for UNESCO action. They reported accounts of programs already in operation throughout the world, and described major issues of theory, along with policies and methods to be used in the attack on illiteracy.

The report concluded with possible steps that UNESCO might take in forwarding a world movement for fundamental education. The first suggestion was that UNESCO serve as a center for the collection and publication of materials that could be utilized by member nations requesting assistance for fundamental education projects. The second suggestion was for the organization of teams that could be sent to various sections of the world to assist member nations in the development of their projects—these teams to learn as well as to teach. The final suggestion was that UNESCO undertake research on problems raised by member states appealing for technical assistance and advice, as well as on problems of a general nature such as those dealing with language, reading materials for new literates, the development of audio-visual aids, financing projects, and the recruitment and preparation of personnel for teaching and administration.

Between 1946 and the present time, UNESCO has followed this blueprint within the limitations of its budget. Out of these experiences certain conclusions have been reached. Foremost is that merely teaching a person to read or write is a victory without meaning unless this new literacy is related to the conditions of life to which the person is bound—his food, his house, his children, his health, and his leisure time.

With knowledges already acquired, UNESCO has developed a world-wide plan to aid its members by helping to train fundamental education workers and by developing teaching materials that they will need in their work. This plan was adopted by the unanimous vote of its sixty-four members at the Sixth Session of the UNESCO General Conference, which met at Paris in June and July of 1951. The plan called for a twelve-year program in which training centers would be established in Equatorial Africa, the Middle East, Latin America, India, and the Far East.

In May 1951, UNESCO opened its first regional center at Patzcuaro, Mexico. The establishment of the Patzcuaro project illustrates international cooperation at its best. The government of Mexico provided the labor and materials to remodel the villa donated as headquarters for the project by ex-President Lazaro Cardenas. Although UNESCO is responsible for the administration of the center, four other international organizations, as well as the government of Mexico, contribute to its support and operation. These include the World Health Organization, the International Labor Organization, the Food and Agriculture Organization, and the Organization of American States. This latter organization was established at the Ninth International Conference of American States held at Bogota, Colombia, in 1948. Part of its program is directed toward technical education that may be shared in by all Latin-American nations.

Fifty-two students from the nine Latin-American countries of Bolivia, Costa Rica, Ecuador, Salvador, Honduras, Peru, Guatemala, Haiti, and Mexico were the first pupils at Patzcuaro. When the Center opened, it was staffed by three UNESCO fundamental education specialists, and five specialists in health and home economics, rural arts and crafts, nutrition, and extension services, provided by FAO, WHO, and ILO.

In keeping with the directive of the UNESCO Conference, the major objectives were to train these students as teachers of fundamental education and to produce instructional materials best suited to fundamental education problems in the Patzcuaro region.

The twenty villages around Lake Patzcuaro serve as a laboratory, since here are found conditions similar to those that will confront the students upon returning home. After a week of sharing experiences gained in their individual countries, followed by a period of basic training in the principles, aims, and methods of fundamental education, the students are divided into teams and move into their assigned villages. Here they study all aspects of village life. Each team maps out a fundamental education program for its assigned community, and then proceeds to carry it out. The students thus gain practical experience in fundamental education while at the same time helping the villagers to make a better life for themselves.

Side by side with these field activities, the students devote time to the production of materials. These include posters, filmstrips, and plays designed to arouse the villagers' interest; primers for the teaching of beginning readers; and more advanced materials for those who have mastered the first steps. The students put all these materials to the test by using them in their actual work in the villages.

The fifty-two students in the first class at Patzcuaro were graduated in November 1952. They returned to their own lands to introduce programs of fundamental education by training others in the techniques they had learned. The second class to enter the Patzcuaro Center numbered one hundred; their course of study will cover twenty-one months. When one realizes that there are 55,000,000 people in Latin America who are illiterate, the magnitude of the task becomes apparent. The important consideration is that the work has *begun*. What has been learned at Patzcuaro by students and staff alike is a beginning toward the challenging goal of bringing a better life to the illiterate half of the world's population.

UNESCO has devised a plan whereby the peoples of the world may share in the work being done at Patzcuaro and other fundamental-education centers. Through the UNESCO gift-coupon plan, groups can participate directly in programs of international assistance by adopting a Voluntary International Assistance project. These projects are items considered important for the ongoing work of the centers, but which are beyond the existing budgetary means. The projects at Patzcuaro range in price from $10 for the purchase of books on hygiene and sanitation to $3,500 for a heavy-duty vehicle chassis.

From these workshops in fundamental education, UNESCO is sending out students upon whom rests the responsibility of taking the first practical steps toward establishing systems of universal education adapted to the cultural and economic needs of each country. And in universal education lies one of the best of all hopes for increasing international understanding.

UNITED NATIONS EDUCATIONAL, SCIENTIFIC AND CULTURAL ORGANIZATION: UNESCO

International Headquarters:
   19 Avenue Kléber, Paris 16, France

Origin

The Conference for the Establishment of an Educational, Scientific and Cultural Organization was convened by the government of the United Kingdom in association with the government of France. Such a conference had been suggested at several meetings of the Conference of Allied Ministers of Education held in London during the war, and was further recommended at the Conference of San Francisco that drafted the United Nations Charter. The Conference met at London from November 1 to 16, 1945.

Discussions were based upon a draft constitution prepared by the Allied Ministers of Education. The Conference, at which the governments of forty-three members of the United Nations were represented, drafted and adopted the United Nations Educational, Scientific and Cultural Organization (UNESCO) Constitution. The Constitution became effective on November 4, 1946. An agreement between the United Nations and UNESCO recognized the latter as a specialized agency on December 14, 1946.

Purpose

UNESCO's purpose is stated in Article I of its Constitution.

The purpose of the Organization is to contribute to peace and security by promoting collaboration among the nations through education, science and culture in order to further universal respect for justice, for the rule of law and for the human rights and fundamental freedoms which are affirmed for the peoples of the world, without distinction of race, sex, language or religion, by the Charter of the United Nations.

Functions

To realize its purpose, UNESCO is charged with the following responsibilities:

a. Collaborate in the work of advancing the mutual knowledge and understanding of peoples, through all means of mass communication and to that end recommend such international agreements as may be necessary to promote the free flow of ideas by word and image;

b. Give fresh impulse to popular education and to the spread of culture;
> by collaborating with Members, at their request, in the development of educational activities;
> by instituting collaboration among the nations to advance the ideal of equality of educational opportunity without regard to race, sex or any distinctions, economic or social;
> by suggesting educational methods best suited to prepare the children of the world for the responsibilities of freedom;

c. Maintain, increase, and diffuse knowledge;
> by assuring the conservation and protection of the world's inheritance of books, works of art and monuments of history and science, and recommending to the nations concerned the necessary international convention; by encouraging cooperation among the nations in all branches of intellectual activity, including the international exchange of persons active in the fields of education, science and culture and the exchange of publications, objects of artistic and scientific interest and other materials of information;
> by initiating methods of international cooperation calculated to give the people of all countries access to the printed and published materials produced by any of them.

Article I concludes with an important reservation concerning the implementation of UNESCO's purpose.

With a view to preserving the independence, integrity and fruitful diversity of the cultures and educational systems of the States members of this Organization, the Organization is prohibited from intervening in matters which are essentially within their domestic jurisdiction.

Membership

As of May 1, 1954, seventy nations were members of UNESCO. A complete list of members appears in the Appendix.

Membership in the United Nations carries with it the right to membership in UNESCO. States not members of the UN may be admitted to UNESCO upon recommendation of the Executive Board and by a two-thirds majority vote of the General Conference. Members who are suspended by the United Nations may, upon UN request, be suspended from UNESCO. Members expelled by the UN automatically cease to be members of UNESCO.

Article VII of UNESCO's Constitution obligates members to make arrangements for the purpose of bringing its own groups interested in educational, scientific, and cultural matters into association with UNESCO. A joint resolution of the Congress, approved July 30, 1946, provided for United States membership in UNESCO and authorized the establishment of a U. S. National Commission for UNESCO.

Recommendations and international conventions adopted by the General Conference of UNESCO are inoperative in any member state unless approved by appropriate authority. However, such recommendations and international conventions are to be submitted to such appropriate authority within one year of the closing of the Conference that adopted same.

Structure and Organization

UNESCO is operated by a General Conference, an Executive Board, the Director-General, and the Secretariat.

THE CONFERENCE

The General Conference is the governing body of UNESCO and

iss Predard Garcia (Ecuadorian student) lking to a villager of Jaracuaro who has en persuaded to install a high hearth instead cooking on the floor.

Inoculation of pigs against cholera. This team has succeeded in reducing cases of cholera by 90 per cent through vaccination.

A student shows a peasant from Opopeo, a mountain village near Patzcuaro, how to graft pear shoots on to a crab-apple tree.

age and home industries can help to raise conomic level of the village. Here instruc- is being given in straw-plaiting.

A modern harvester dragged by a bullock team, a typical combination of old and new.

Groups of small farmers have joined together in cooperative associations to buy and use some of the agricultural machinery which was financed by the International Bank's $5 million loan to Colombia's Caja de Credito.

New areas are being added to the usable farm land of Colombia.

Tractor drivers who will use the agricultural equipment learn practical operating details from experienced teachers.

is composed of one representative from each member state. Each nation has one vote in the General Conference, which meets at least once every two years. The General Conference reviews the work of UNESCO and approves the budget for the next financial year.

THE EXECUTIVE BOARD

The Executive Board consists of eighteen members elected by the General Conference for a term of three years. Six new members are elected each year. The members serve as private individuals, not as representatives of their respective countries, and no more than one national of any member state may serve on the Board at the same time.

THE SECRETARIAT

The program decided upon by the General Conference is carried out by an international Secretariat with its headquarters in Paris. Head of the Secretariat is the Director-General, nominated by the Executive Board and appointed by the General Conference.

Activities

The seven main departments of the UNESCO Secretariat indicate the areas with which this workshop deals: Education, Natural Sciences, Social Sciences, Cultural Activities, Exchange of Persons, Mass Communication, Technical Assistance. The Secretariat serves as a clearing house for knowledge in these various fields that can then be shared among nations.

The effectiveness of such a clearing house can best be achieved if publications and other materials of information can circulate freely between nations. To accomplish this purpose, the General Conference at its fifth session in 1950 unanimously adopted an agreement aimed at reducing the tariff and trade barriers to the free international exchange of knowledge. On May 21, 1952, this treaty became effective upon its ratification by the tenth nation—Sweden. By July 1,

1953, fourteen nations had approved the agreement. As of that date the United States had not ratified this treaty.

The agreement ends custom duties on books, magazines, painting, sculpture, travel literature, maps, musical scores, museum materials, and articles for the blind. It provides for the duty-free import of educational films and other audio-visual materials consigned to recognized cultural institutions. In addition, participating countries agree to promote the free flow of educational, scientific, and cultural material. This is the first treaty to become effective under UNESCO sponsorship.

UNESCO has taken the initiative in forming international organizations responsible for cultural exchanges among nations. Typical of these are the International Theatre Institute, the International Council of Museums, and the International Music Council. Meetings of experts are convened by UNESCO for the purpose of sharing educational, scientific, and cultural knowledge. Papers prepared by these specialists are distributed from Paris and by national commissions interested in UNESCO's work.

UNESCO educational missions are available to those nations wishing to extend free and compulsory education. UNESCO has set up schools for Arab refugee children in the Near East, and is engaged in the reconstruction of educational facilities in the Republic of Korea.

UNESCO has established field science offices to serve the underdeveloped areas of the world. These offices act as clearing houses and coordination centers for scientific experimentation and publication in their respective areas. Visiting scientists lecture at these centers and often select candidates for scientific training abroad. Schools, farm groups, industrialists, and research workers are able to contact specialists in other countries through UNESCO field science offices.

In carrying out activities designed to implement its purpose

UNESCO is, in effect, pioneering. Never before has an international organization been called upon to develop techniques for constructing the defenses of peace in the minds of men while honoring and preserving the independence and integrity of its members. Promoting understanding among neighborhoods through education, science, and culture will produce no sensational blows for immediate peace, but it *will* produce solid blows for a lasting peace.

A page from a reading primer produced by the students at the Center for use in the village schools.

e s a

mano mono
mano mono

no es mono, es mano

esa mano

esas manos

8
BANK

TRACTORS AND TOOLS

*The International Bank for
Reconstruction and Development*

ON THE MORNING OF JUNE 25, 1946, the most unusual bank in the world opened its offices for business.

One of the unique features of this bank was that its stock was owned by *governments*. These governments realized that the poverty of a few countries could be a serious threat to the peace of all. They also realized that the best way to eliminate poverty is by helping people help themselves through productive effort. But creating tools, plants, and jobs that make productive effort possible takes money. So the governments agreed that providing the capital necessary for such projects—either through new enterprise or through replacing and rebuilding enterprises devastated during World War II —should be the aim of this new bank.

Thus the International Bank for Reconstruction and Development (Bank) became unique in another respect: its dedication to raising the standard of living of the peoples who lived in its member nations. This was to be done by making loans to member countries that had plans for productive enterprise but could not get money either at home or from private investors in other lands.

This latter point is most important. The Bank was not designed to compete with private investors. The Bank was to make loans only when member states could prove that private financing was not to be had. On the other hand, the Bank was designed to cooperate with private investors by making it possible for them to buy bonds

A World Bank loan of $16.5 million is financing
extensive highway repair and reconstruction.

Many of Colombia's roads twist and turn across mountainous terrain and part of the Bank's loan is financing
the regrading of such stretches. Fuel dumps, supply
offices, and maintenance bases have been established
at regular intervals on roads under repair.

The La Insula generating plant is one of the three
small hydroelectric stations which the Bank is helping
finance in Colombia. For this plant, which supplies
power for Manizales, the Bank has loaned $2.6 million.
Manizales is an important industrial and commercial
center in the heart of the coffee-growing region.

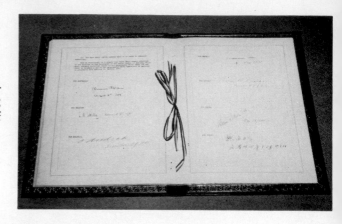

The Articles of Agreement, International Monetary Fund, showing the signatures of representatives of Member governments.

Camille Gutt of Belgium and the Secretary-General of the United Nations sign the International Monetary Fund Protocol, 1948.

With this scroll the Government of Honduras expressed appreciation of the Fund's technical assistance in establishing the country's first central bank.

guaranteed by the Bank. Private investors could participate in the development of productive enterprises by relying upon the Bank's good judgment in making loans.

This is an account of how one Bank member—Colombia—utilized the Bank's resources to build a better life for her people.

During World War II, Colombia was unable to buy heavy farm equipment in the international markets. This meant that fewer crops were raised, although at the same time Colombia's population was growing, and she needed more food. The money that she earned in foreign markets had to be spent on importing foodstuffs and staples, and so there was no money to purchase the tractors and tools from countries that manufactured this equipment.

This posed a hard question for the people of Colombia, and they did some hard thinking about it. They first took account of their own resources and found that they just didn't have the dollars with which to buy agricultural machinery. They explored the private international financing markets, but found no opportunity there. Even with this situation confronting them, however, the people of Colombia were not without hope. Their government was a member of the International Bank for Reconstruction and Development. Perhaps this might be a productive enterprise of interest to the Bank.

But members just don't approach the Bank and ask for a loan. The World Bank expects its borrowers to have a sound plan worked out for the use of its money, just as any other bank does. Colombia had to work out such a plan.

There is a bank in Colombia that has long specialized in loans to farmers: the Caja de Credito Agrario, Industrial y Minero, better known as the Caja. This is an official bank that was founded in 1931. Its Board of Directors includes representatives of the Central Bank, the Central Mortgage Bank, the Federation of Coffee Growers, the Society of Agriculturists, and other important interests. The Caja has a total capital of 100,000,000 Colombian pesos. The Caja makes loans to farmers at rates lower than those charged by commercial banks. A farmer can borrow as little as 50 pesos from any of the many branches of the Caja.

In addition to lending money, the Caja encourages agricultural development through two of its departments: the Department of Agricultural Provision and the Department of Agricultural Development. The Department of Agricultural Provision helps farmers finance the purchase of farm equipment. This Department also provides instruction in the proper use of farm machinery.

With this experience as a guide the authorities of the Caja surveyed the country's most pressing needs in heavy farm equipment—tractors and tools. It was estimated that $5,000,000 was needed to bridge the immediate production gap. Should this money be forthcoming from the World Bank, the Caja was not only prepared to guarantee the loan but was prepared to allocate the tractors and tools to those areas where productive results seemed most promising and where, in addition, instruction for the proper use of the equipment could be provided. The plan was drawn accordingly.

Even though the thoroughgoing preparation of the plan and the lack of private financing indicated that this loan might be of interest to the World Bank, neither the government of Colombia nor the Caja made a formal application for a loan. After all, what the Caja thought of this investment and what the Executive Directors of the International Bank *might* think of it were two different things.

As a result, the facts and figures that had been gathered at home were transmitted to the Colombian Embassy in Washington. Officials at the Embassy communicated the Caja's interest in this proposition to the Bank on an informal basis. The Bank examined the Caja's plan, and decided its soundness warranted sending a technician to Colombia to study the situation at first hand.

This technician was Dr. J. Thompson Lund, an agricultural engineer with broad experience in the United States and in other countries. He is particularly well qualified in the field of tropical agriculture, and has made field studies in India, Chile, Peru, and Pakistan.

Following a survey of the situation, Dr. Lund concluded that Colombia could productively use $5,000,000 worth of agricultural equipment if provision were made for replacements. He further suggested that 20 per cent by value be sold for cash, 60 per cent by value be sold on credit, and the remaining 20 per cent or a part thereof be sold to the Ministry of Agriculture for use on special operations. His report confirmed this project to be a sound one both technically and economically.

Back at the offices of the Bank, Dr. Lund's report was studied by a working party made up of representatives of the chief operating departments of the Bank. The working party then passed its recommendations to the Staff Loan Committee, made up of the President, Vice-President, Assistant to the President, and other senior officers of the Bank. After a favorable review by this Committee, the President recommended the loan to the Executive Directors, who approved it.

The formal application for the loan was made by the Colombian government, speaking for the Caja. The terms of the loan called for ten semiannual installments of $500,000 each, due on the 15th of May and the 15th of November. Payments were to start in 1952 (the loan was completed on August 19, 1949) and to continue through 1956. The Caja has met all its obligations to date on this note, which will be completely paid on November 15, 1956. Interest is at the rate of 3½ per cent.

Upon receipt of the loan, the Caja went into the international market to make its purchases. Most of the loan was used to import heavy, medium, and light tractors. Much of the equipment was purchased in the United States from such firms as Caterpillar, Allis-Chalmers, and International Harvester. Some of the tractors were purchased in Canada from Massey-Harris and Company. The smaller tools were purchased from a number of firms in the United States. Thus the dollars intended for productive use in Colombia played a productive role outside that country also by creating needs that were satisfied by workers and capital far removed from South America.

When this equipment arrived in Colombia, the terms of agreement were met by the Caja. The central office of the Caja sent experts to the parts of the country where the Bank-financed tractors and tools were being used by Colombia's farmers. In addition to their own expert instruction, the Caja made arrangements with the International Harvester Company to send four instructors to Colombia. These instructors went into the fields to demonstrate the most effective means of operating and caring for the equipment.

On a follow-up visit (regular Bank policy), Dr. Lund observed some of the tractor-training schools that had been established by the Caja. He reported that the instruction was equal to any he had seen anywhere.

Out in the Tolima, Cauca, and Cundinamarca regions of Colombia, these new tractors and tools are hard at work on the land. In addition, two new regions, the valleys of Sinu and San Jorge, are being added to the usable farm land of Colombia. Into these areas have come colonists. Along with the equipment furnished by the Bank, and the know-how furnished by the Caja, these sturdy people are furnishing the enthusiasm that comes from opportunity. Together they are producing for peace.

INTERNATIONAL BANK FOR RECONSTRUCTION AND DEVELOPMENT: BANK

International Headquarters:
1818 H Street, N.W., Washington 25, D.C.

Origin

The Articles of Agreement of the Bank were drawn up by the United Nations Monetary and Financial Conference at Bretton Woods, N.H., in July 1944. The Bank came into existence on December 27, 1945, when its Articles of Agreement were signed by twenty-eight governments. After an inaugural meeting of its Board of Governors held at Savannah, Ga., in March 1946, at which its first Board of Executive Directors was elected, the Bank officially began operations in Washington, D.C., on June 25, 1946. On April 15, 1947, the Bank opened an office in New York City from which its marketing operations are directed. On November 15, 1947, the Bank became a Specialized Agency cooperating with the United Nations.

Purposes

The purposes of the Bank are stated in Article I of the Articles of Agreement:

I To assist in the reconstruction and development of territories of members by facilitating the investment of capital for productive purposes, including the restoration of economies destroyed or disrupted by war, the reconversion of productive facilities to peacetime needs and the encouragement of the development of productive facilities and resources in less developed countries.

II To promote private foreign investment by means of guarantees or participations in loans and other investments made by private investors; and when private capital is not

available on reasonable terms, to supplement private investment by providing, on suitable conditions, finance for productive purposes out of its own capital, funds raised by it
and its other resources.

III To promote the long-range balanced growth of international trade and the maintenance of equilibrium in balances of payments by encouraging international investment
for the development of the productive resources of members,
thereby assisting in raising productivity, the standard of living and conditions of labor in their territories.

IV To arrange the loans made or guaranteed by it in
relation to international loans through other channels so that
the more useful and urgent projects, large and small alike,
will be dealt with first.

V To conduct its operations with due regard to the effect of international investment on business conditions in
the territories of members and, in the immediate post-war
years, to assist in bringing about a smooth transition from
a wartime to a peacetime economy.

Functions

The major functions of the Bank are included in various Articles
of the Articles of Agreement:

The resources and the facilities of the Bank shall be
used exclusively for the benefit of members with equitable
consideration to projects for development and projects for
reconstruction alike. . . . .

When the member in whose territories the project is located is not itself the borrower, the member or the central
bank or some comparable agency of the member which is
acceptable to the Bank, fully guarantees the repayment of

the principal and the payment of interest and other charges on the loan.

The Bank is satisfied that in the prevailing market conditions the borrower would be unable otherwise to obtain the loan under conditions which in the opinion of the Bank are reasonable for the borrower.

A competent committee, as provided for in Article V, Section 7, has submitted a written report recommending the project after a careful study of the merits of the proposal.

In the opinion of the Bank the rate of interest and other charges are reasonable and such rate, charges and the schedule for repayment of principal are appropriate to the project. . . .

In guarantecing a loan made by other investors, the Bank receives suitable compensation for its risk. . . . .

The Bank may make or facilitate loans which satisfy the general conditions of Article III in any of the following ways:

> By making or participating in direct loans out of its own funds corresponding to its unimpaired paid-up capital and surplus and, subject to Section 6 of this Article, to its reserves.

> By making or participating in direct loans out of funds raised in the market of a member, or otherwise borrowed by the Bank.

> By guaranteeing in whole or in part loans made by private investors through the usual investment channels.

Members and Capital

The original members of the Bank were members of the International Monetary Fund which accepted membership in the Bank before January 1, 1946. Subsequent membership required a nation to be a member of the Fund, and at such terms as the Bank might prescribe. As of May 1, 1954, the Bank had fifty-five members. A complete list of members is included in the Appendix.

The authorized capital stock of the Bank is $10,000,000,000 in terms of United States dollars of the weight and fineness in effect on July 1, 1944. This stock is divided into 100,000 shares of $100,000 each, available only to members. Subscriptions were allotted among those nations attending the United Nations Monetary and Financial Conference in July 1944.

Trade figures, reserves, national income, and other considerations determined a nation's subscription. A total of $9,100,000,000 in subscriptions were set up in "Schedule A" of the Articles of Agreement, ranging from $200,000 for Panama to $3,175,000,000 for the United States.

The Bank's operating expenses are met from net earnings. As a result there is no need to assess each member for a proportion of the annual budget. After paying its operating expenses during its first year of operation, the Bank had a deficit of nearly a million dollars. In its fifth year of operation, after meeting expenses, the Bank had net earnings of $15,000,000. Earnings are placed in a general reserve fund. Commissions on loans are placed in a Special Reserve. By the middle of 1952 the Bank had total reserves of over $80,000,000.

Members may be suspended from the Bank by a majority vote of the Governors. Any nation that ceases to be a member of the International Monetary Fund automatically ceases to be a member of the Bank after three months, unless permitted to remain a member by three-fourths of the total voting power.

Members may withdraw from the Bank. After satisfying certain conditions established in the Articles of Agreement, members who withdraw receive back their original subscription plus a share of the Bank's earnings during their membership. Poland withdrew from the Bank in 1950 and received a dividend of $341,222.03.

Structure and Organization

The Bank has a Board of Governors, Executive Directors, a President and staff.

THE BOARD OF GOVERNORS

All powers of the Bank are vested in a Board of Governors consisting of a representative appointed for a five-year term by each member country. Each Governor has an Alternate who may act in his absence. The Board selects its Chairman annually. Each member has two hundred and fifty votes, plus one additional vote for each share of capital stock held by the nation he represents.

THE EXECUTIVE DIRECTORS

The Board of Governors has delegated most of its powers to the Executive Directors. Each Executive Director also has an Alternate. Five Executive Directors are appointed by the five largest stockholders (the United States, the United Kingdom, France, China, and India). The other Executive Directors are elected by the Governors of the remaining members, so that each of the elected Directors usually represents a number of countries. Executive Directors are appointed or elected every two years.

THE PRESIDENT

The President is *ex officio* Chairman of the Executive Directors without vote except in case of a tie. He is elected by the Executive Directors and is the chief executive officer of the Bank. He is responsible for the conduct of the business of the Bank and for the organization, appointment, and dismissal of its officers and staff. Under him, the Vice-President acts as general manager, with responsibility for assuring the effective operation of the other offices and departments. The Bank's staff, under the supervision of the President and

Vice-President, is responsible for the general operations of the Bank and for formulating policy recommendations for submission to the President.

Activities

The Bank's loans are financed from two sources: the stock subscriptions of member governments and the sale of bonds in the private markets. As one of the Bank's aims is to encourage private funds in international investment, the marketing of bonds is an important activity. The Bank has sold well over $600,000,000 worth of bonds. Although over 90 per cent of this total represents sales in the United States market, Bank bonds have also been sold in the markets of Britain, Canada, and Switzerland.

The Bank has made loans for varying purposes in many countries. Credit Nationale in France applied loan funds to presses for automobile factories, equipment for steel mills, airplanes for Air France, port rehabilitation, railroad locomotives, and agricultural equipment.

Four private shipping companies in the Netherlands used Bank funds to purchase cargo vessels and modernize equipment. The Kingdom of Denmark utilized Bank funds to repair and replace agricultural and industrial equipment damaged during the Occupation. A loan of $24,100,000 was used by the Federal Electricity Commission of Mexico to purchase equipment essential to a power-expansion program.

Part of a $75,000,000 loan to the Brazilian Traction, Light and Power Company was used for new telephone plant and equipment. Belgium used a Bank loan to import equipment for two steel mills. Yugoslavia borrowed $2,700,000 to finance the purchase of timber equipment.

The Bank aims to help the neighborhoods of the world help themselves to a higher production of goods and services—which in turn will lead to a higher standard of living and provide a firm basis for peace.

9
FUND

THE FUND AND THE FRANC

International Monetary Fund

ONE OF THE COMMON MISCONCEPTIONS that most of us have is that we pay with money for goods and services produced by others. Actually, we pay for these goods and services with other goods and services. The money with which we buy things is worth only as much as the goods and services it represents to the person from whom we purchase. When we carry on routine transactions within our own country, we don't give much thought to this "real" value of money. We accept payment in money from others, and expect them to accept ours, because we have a common knowledge of what the money is worth in terms of butter or battleships.

But when we carry on transactions outside our own national boundaries, new factors enter into our calculations. We must first concern ourselves with the amount of goods and services that we can purchase with the *foreign currency we accept in payment,* and secondly with *what kinds* of goods and services this foreign currency will buy. With the increasing dependence of any one world neighborhood upon the goods and services produced in another, it is important that international monetary cooperation exist.

The International Monetary Fund was created so that countries could exchange their pounds, dollars, francs and pesos for goods and services produced in other countries, and at the same time have confidence in the value of the money received in terms of other goods and services.

To make a plan of this kind work, certain conditions must exist. Nations must agree to refrain from undesirable trade practices. They must work toward the free exchange of national currencies. They must make an attempt to establish consistent (par) values for their currencies in terms of gold or some other recognized standard. They must establish means whereby nations with temporary exchange difficulties may buy other national currency with which they can purchase goods and services. Finally, they must have an intergovernmental organization through which the member nations may learn of problems in international exchange and take both individual and collective measures to solve them.

The Articles of Agreement of the International Monetary Fund that were drafted by the delegates to the United Nations Monetary and Financial Conference at Bretton Woods, New Hampshire, on July 22, 1944, provided a framework within which international monetary cooperation might be promoted. The way in which this cooperation has developed can probably best be understood by following its relations with a member nation.

Belgium has a population slightly in excess of nine million, residing in an area approximately the size of the state of Maryland. The Belgian people virtually live by foreign trade. A third of their food must be imported, as well as all the raw materials essential to their industries, with the exception of coal. To pay for these goods and services, the people of Belgium must export 35 per cent of their entire national production to other lands.

Because Belgium is a comparatively small nation, her money does not exert a great influence on international markets. The Belgians must therefore be able to depend upon buying goods and services for their own use with the money they receive from their exports. If they are unable to buy the things they need with the money their international customers pay them, then their very existence is threatened.

As a trading nation, it was only natural that Belgium sent a delegation to the Bretton Woods Conference and that this delegation played an important role in drafting the purposes and functions for the Fund. When Belgium joined the Fund on December 27, 1945, it formally agreed to accept the privileges and responsibilities of membership in an organization it had helped create.

The Bretton Woods Conference established a monetary fund for the purpose of facilitating international exchange transactions. The Fund was set at $8,800,000,000, and each nation was assigned a quota for payment based upon a study of its international trade figures, gold reserves, national income, and other considerations. Belgium's share was set at $225,000,000.

The Articles of Agreement provided that quotas were to be paid partially in gold (or gold and U.S. dollars) and partially in the members' currency. The official par value for each national currency was fixed by agreement with the Fund prior to the quota payments. On December 18, 1946, the Fund agreed to the official par value of the Belgian franc as being 43.8275 francs per U.S. dollar. As the very financial foundation of the Fund depends upon the stability of the par values of the participating currencies, the members are committed by the Articles of Agreement to make no change in the par value of their currency without consultation with the Fund. The Fund makes a study of proposed changes to determine their impact upon international exchange and the stability of the Fund. Under these conditions the par value of the franc was subsequently established, on September 22, 1949, at 50.12 Belgian francs per U.S. dollar.

Under its original par value rate of 43.8275 francs per U.S. dollar the Belgian Government subscribed to its quota with $22,500 in U.S. dollars, $56,227,500 in gold, and $168,750,000 in its own currency. The gold and dollars were transferred outside Belgium to a depository bank named by the Fund. The $168,750,000 in Belgian francs was deposited at the Banque Nationale de Belgique S.A. in the form of non-interest-bearing, non-negotiable notes that may be called for by the Fund at any time.

On March 1, 1947, the first Managing Director of the Fund, Mr. Camille Gutt of Belgium, announced that the Fund was ready to conduct exchange transactions. These transactions are subject to the approval of the Executive Directors, who meet in Washington as often as the business of the Fund requires. The Executive Directors select the Managing Director, who is chief of the operating staff of the Fund and who conducts the affairs of the Fund under the direction of the Executive Directors.

As in any other financial institution, the affairs of members in their dealings with the Fund are considered confidential. The transactions that are described in the following paragraphs are a matter of public record, but the *reasons* for the transactions are based upon assumptions drawn from sources outside the Fund.

Since the end of World War II, the balance of trade between Belgium and the United States has constantly been in favor of the United States. This situation reached a peak in 1947, when the United States sold $516,920,000 in goods to Belgium and bought $61,781,000 in return. This left an important dollar deficit of $455,-139,000 for Belgium, and posed some very real problems for people who must trade to maintain their standard of living.

One of the ways in which the Belgian government attempted to meet this problem was through currency purchases from the Fund that would help it meet its most pressing obligations. The Executive Directors of the Fund approved a sale of 33,000,000 U.S. dollars to the Belgian Government for francs. The actual purchase took place in late 1947 and in the early months of 1948. This meant that the Fund increased its holdings of Belgian francs by $33,000,000 and reduced its holdings of U.S. dollars by a similar amount.

Another way in which the Belgian government attempted to reduce its dollar deficit was by increased sales of goods to other countries. Two of Belgium's important customers have been the Netherlands and Norway. In 1947 Belgium exported $164,034,000 in goods to the Netherlands and imported goods worth $114,439,000. The value of Belgian goods exported to Norway in 1947 was $46,-055,000, and the value of goods received was $19,125,000. In these instances the Netherlands and Norway had important franc deficits with Belgium.

To offset these deficits, Norway and the Netherlands utilized their privilege of membership in the Fund and requested purchases of Belgian francs. This request was subsequently honored by the Executive Directors. In May 1948 the Netherlands purchased 300,000,000 Belgian francs with guilders; during June and July, Norway purchased 200,000,000 Belgian francs with her currency, the krone. The total of these purchases amounted to $11,400,000. As in Belgium's request, these two members stated that the francs were needed in a current payments difficulty and that they would be used in accordance with the Fund Agreement.

It should not be inferred from these transactions that it is the business of the Fund to equalize trade deficits. The year 1947 was a trying one in Western Europe. Agricultural production was far below normal. Traditional sources of supply were no longer open to these nations. Because of the bad harvests they turned to the Western Hemisphere for food products. These purchases, added to their normal import of other goods, led to an increased deficit with the West. In 1947 the countries of Western Europe had a total deficit of $7,500,-000,000 with countries in the Western Hemisphere. As this amount approaches the total currencies available to the Fund, it is obvious that the Fund was providing temporary assistance for specific emergencies in Belgium, Norway, and the Netherlands.

On each of these transactions the Fund collected a fee. On the $33,000,000 purchased by Belgium the charge was ¾ of 1 per cent. From charges on transactions the Fund is able to meet its operating expenses, and as a result no annual contribution is made by the members of this Specialized Agency.

Since purchases from the Fund are considered to be of a temporary nature, the Articles of Agreement provide that nations who have used their own currency to purchase other currency from the Fund shall repurchase their own currency with either gold or a currency that can be utilized by all members. At the end of the Fund's financial year all members submit a report on their monetary reserves. A nation's monetary reserve is defined by the Articles of Agreement as its holdings of gold, convertible currencies of other members, and the currencies of such non-members as the Fund may specify. Using the monetary reserve as a base, the Fund decides the repurchase obligations of members who have purchased currency. If this were not the case, the Fund's resources might become frozen by virtue of the fact that the Fund would have no easily convertible currency available for purchase by other members. The Fund's general rule is that repurchases should take place within a period not exceeding three to five years.

Through April 30, 1951, the Belgian Government repurchased $21,585,706.75 worth of Belgian francs from the Fund with gold and U.S. dollars. This amount took into account an increase in Belgium's reserve holdings, as well as the reduction of the Fund's holding of Belgian francs resulting from the purchases made by Norway and the Netherlands.

Because of these repurchases and the fact that Belgium had followed policies that were in accord with the Fund's purposes, the Executive Board of the Fund granted Belgium a stand-by arrangement of $50,000,000 on June 19, 1952. Under this new policy adopted by the Board on February 13, 1952, a member may be given the right to purchase other currency during a specified period of time. This gives the member an opportunity to do advance planning in international

The Headquarters of the International Monetary Fund in Washington, D .C.

President Aleman of Mexico addressing the Seventh Annual Meeting of the Fund's Board of Governors in Mexico City.

The Deputy Secretary of the Fund welcomes technical assistance trainees from the Philippines, India, Thailand, and Iran.

A weather balloon is inflated and equipped with a radiosonde, in the white box at right.

Analyzing weather bulletins for broadcast to shipping. Bulletins comprise weather forecasts, storm warnings, and analyses as issued by Forecast and Analysis Centers.

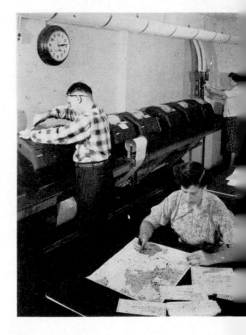

Analyzing surface and upper air charts preparatory to issuing weather forecasts and advices at a typical District Weather Forecasting Office.

trade that would not be possible if the member lacked convertible currency. For this service a slightly higher fee is charged if the currency is actually purchased. The stand-by agreements are renewable for specified periods of time, and mark constructive new possibilities in international monetary cooperation.

In addition to the transactions discussed above, the Fund attempts to coordinate the policies of countries which have common problems to solve. The annual meeting of the Fund provides all members an opportunity to raise questions they consider to be within the province of the Fund. At the 1952 meeting the Governor for Belgium, Maurice Frere, invited the Board of Governors to charge the Executive Board with the responsibility of studying certain exchange practices which his government felt were detrimental to the spirit and purpose of the Fund. A resolution to this effect directed the Executive Board to make a detailed study of these practices during 1953.

The seven years in which the Fund has been operating have been chaotic ones in world trade. The adjustments following the war created difficulties that were intensified by the closing of certain traditional markets, inflation, trade restrictions, and the tendencies of some countries to concentrate on selling in one or two markets. Even under normal circumstances the establishment of a sound system of international payments is an exacting one that demands the confidence, good will, and integrity of all nations.

During these seven years the Fund has had to develop techniques designed to provide a practical basis for its operations. Where the Fund's efforts have been matched by a corresponding practicality on the part of its members, the results have been constructive. Belgium's relations with the Fund are cases in point. As the neighborhoods of the world strive toward reducing the barriers to the exchange of goods and services among them, they will find in the Fund an experienced workshop for facilitating this trade.

INTERNATIONAL MONETARY FUND: FUND

International Headquarters:
1818 H Street, N.W., Washington 6, D.C.

Origin

In May 1944, the President of the United States issued invitations to forty-four United and Associated Nations to attend a monetary conference at Bretton Woods, New Hampshire, in July 1944. On June 15 a group of United States financial experts assembled at Atlantic City, New Jersey, and were joined a few days later by representatives of fifteen nations for a preliminary meeting. The Bretton Woods conference of July 1-22 (formally referred to as the United Nations Monetary and Financial Conference) produced the Articles of Agreement for the International Monetary Fund (Fund) and for the International Bank for Reconstruction and Development.

The Fund's actual existence as an international organization began on December 27, 1945, when governments contributing 80 per cent of the monetary quotas set at Bretton Woods signed the Articles of Agreement. The first organizational meeting of the Board of Governors was convened at Savannah, Georgia, on March 8, 1946. On December 18, 1946, the Fund announced its agreement to the official par values for the currencies of thirty-two of its members, and it began operations on March 1, 1947, with a public declaration that it was ready to conduct exchange transactions.

Purposes

The purposes of the Fund are set forth in Article I of the Articles of Agreement, as follows:

i. To promote international monetary cooperation through a permanent institution which provides the machinery for consultation and collaboration on international monetary problems.

ii. To facilitate the expansion and balanced growth of international trade, and to contribute thereby to the promotion and maintenance of high levels of employment and real income and to the development of the productive resources of all members as primary objectives of economic policy.

iii. To promote exchange stability, to maintain orderly exchange arrangements among members, and to avoid competitive exchange depreciation.

iv. To assist in the establishment of a multilateral system of payments in respect of current transactions between members and in the elimination of foreign exchange restrictions which hamper the growth of world trade.

v. To give confidence to members by making the Fund's resources available to them under adequate safeguards, thus providing them with opportunity to correct maladjustments in their balance of payments without resorting to measures destructive of national or international prosperity.

vi. In accordance with the above, to shorten the duration and lessen the degree of disequilibrium in the international balances of payments of members.

Functions

The carrying out of the Fund's purposes depends chiefly upon agreements made by the members to the Fund and upon the consultations of its Executive Directors.

In ratifying the Articles of Agreement the members commit themselves to the following: to refrain from competitive foreign exchange practices, to work toward eliminating restrictions on the exchange of national currencies, to strive toward establishing consistent rates for currencies in terms of gold and the United States dollar, and to consult with the Fund on the proposed national matters in the monetary fields so that these may be studied as to their international impact.

The Executive Directors function in continuous session at Washington and meet as frequently as the business of the Fund demands. In carrying out its responsibilities to the Fund the Directors must constantly weigh the world-wide research and statistical data prepared by the staff. Against this information the Directors determine Fund policy with regard to monetary measures proposed by members. These concern changes in par values, exchange restrictions and gold policies, in addition to requests to purchase other currencies or gold for equivalent amounts of the member's national currency.

Membership, Quotas and Subscriptions

The original members of the Fund were those countries represented at the United Nations Monetary and Financial Conference whose governments deposited instruments of ratification prior to January 1, 1946. Membership is open to other governments under conditions determined by the Fund. As of May 1, 1954, the Fund had fifty-five members. A complete list of members appears in the Appendix. Each member is assigned a quota. Quotas for original members were established by the United Nations Monetary and Financial Conference under Schedule "A" of the Articles of Agreement. These quotas ranged from $500,000 assigned Panama to $2,750,000,000 assigned the United States. Countries admitted to the Fund subsequent to January 1, 1946, are assigned quotas by the Fund. Every five years quotas are reviewed by the Fund and, if necessary, adjustments are made.

Subscriptions to the Fund are paid in gold and in the member's own currency. Twenty-five per cent of the quota (or ten per cent of the member's net holdings of gold and United States dollars if a lesser amount on March 1, 1947) is paid in gold. The balance is paid in the member's own currency. The authorized subscriptions of members as of April 30, 1952, was $8,153,500,000.

Members may withdraw from the Fund by transmitting such notice in writing. Under certain conditions members may be required to withdraw from the Fund.

There are no annual assessments to members. Operating expenses are met from profits. The Fund's income arises out of charges on transactions and interest on excess balances of members' currencies held by the Fund.

Structure and Organization

The Fund has a Board of Governors, a Board of Executive Directors, a Managing Director, and an international staff.

THE BOARD OF GOVERNORS

All powers of the Fund are vested in the Board of Governors, consisting of one Governor and one Alternate appointed by each member. Their terms are for five years, subject to the pleasure of the individual governments.

The Governors may delegate and, in fact, have delegated to the Executive Directors all of their powers except, as provided in Article XII, Section 2, of the Articles of Agreement, the power to:

i. Admit new members and determine the conditions of their admission.

ii. Approve a revision of quotas.

iii. Approve a uniform change in the par value of the currencies of all members.

iv. Make arrangements to cooperate with other international organizations.

v. Determine the distribution of the net income of the Fund.

vi. Require a member to withdraw.

vii. Decide to liquidate the Fund.

viii. Decide appeals from interpretations of this agreement given by the Executive Directors.

The Board of Governors holds an annual meeting and such other meetings as may be called by the Board or by the Executive Directors. The Governors may also vote between meetings by mail or cable. Voting power is approximately proportional to the amount of capital to be contributed to the Fund by each member.

THE EXECUTIVE DIRECTORS

The Executive Directors are responsible for the conduct of the general operations of the Fund, for this purpose exercising all the powers delegated to them by the Board of Governors. They are in permanent session, normally at the headquarters of the Fund.

Five of the Executive Directors are appointed by the five countries with the largest quotas in the Fund. Nine others are elected by the remaining countries, with the provision that the American republics not entitled to appoint Directors are entitled to two of the elective directorships.

Each Executive Director exercises voting power approximately in proportion to the quota contributed by his country, in the instances of the five appointed Directors, and each elected Director casts as a unit all the votes of the countries that elected him. Each Director appoints an Alternate with full power to act for him in his absence.

THE MANAGING DIRECTOR

The Chairman of the Board of Executive Directors is also the

Managing Director of the Fund. He is appointed by the Executive Directors for a term of five years. He acts as Chairman of the Directors' meetings, but has no vote except a deciding vote in case of an equal division. As Managing Director he is chief of the operating staff of the Fund, and conducts, under direction of the Executive Directors, the ordinary business of the Fund. The Executive Directors have provided for a Deputy Managing Director to serve as Acting Chairman of their Board when the Managing Director is absent, and to assist him in administrative matters.

THE STAFF

The staff of the Fund is an international body whose members owe their loyalty and obedience only to the Fund on Fund matters. They are divided into four offices and six departments: Office of Managing Director, Office of the Secretary, Office of Administration, Office of Public Relations, Legal Department, Research Department, Treasurer's Department, and two area departments.

Activities

The Fund's activities are summarized in the annual report of the Executive Directors to the Board of Governors. The report includes a summary of the world economic situation with observations and recommendations, a statement of the use of the Fund's resources, a report on gold production and transactions, and survey of exchange restrictions, par values, and exchange rates.

WINDS AND STORMS

World Meteorological Organization

> *SS Irish Oak* 30476 49918 82709 95555 15142 86200
> 24620 05640 149//

UPON SUCH CODE MESSAGES as this, human life and safety depend. Thousands of similar code messages are the stuff out of which the weather man builds his daily forecasts.

The above message originated on the vessel *Irish Oak* owned by Irish Shipping Limited and operating on the North Atlantic routes. The *Irish Oak* is one of the more than two thousand vessels serving as voluntary observing ships in the World Meteorological Organization (WMO) Ship Reporting Program. Operating under the Commission for Maritime Meteorology of the WMO, the thousands of observations going out from these ships each day provide invaluable synoptic (broad-view) weather data when they are coordinated.

All maritime nations are asked to recruit selected ships, not only to make observations of the weather but to transmit them by radio to various collecting centers. By the middle of 1953 there were more than 2,400 such selected ships recruited by the national meteorological services of twenty-two countries. The United States has 633 such selected ships, among them the *United States,* the *America,* the *Constitution,* and the *Independence.* The *Flying Enterprise* of the Captain Carlson saga was a selected ship.

If a ship's owner agrees to join the weather reporting program, the meteorological service of the country in which the ship is registered lends tested instruments, as recommended by WMO. When the Meteorological Service of Ireland notified WMO in 1952 that the *Irish Oak* had entered the program, they indicated that a mercurial barometer, a sling psychrometer, a sea temperature thermometer, a canvas bucket, and a barograph had been placed aboard the vessel.

No special staff is carried for the purpose of making observations. The work is entirely voluntary and is accomplished by the ships' officers. To insure uniformity in reporting, the Commission for Maritime Meteorology requests that the observations be made at 0001, 0600, 1200, and 1800 Greenwich Mean Time (G.M.T.). If unusual conditions exist, such as a vessel being on the fringes of a hurricane where information may prove invaluable, ships are requested to report each hour.

An analysis of the *Irish Oak* code message indicates the elements that are included in each report.

SS Irish Oak 30476 49918 82709 95555 15142 86200 24620 05640 149//

> *Decode:* Observation of 1800 GCT (Greenwich Civil Time) Tuesday. Position 47.6 N. latitude, 49.9 w. longitude. Sky overcast. Wind direction 270 (w), speed 9 knots. Visibility 1 mile. Weather, drizzle, continuous and thick but not freezing. Weather during the preceding six hours, mostly drizzle. Barometric pressure 1015.1 millibars. Temperature 42 degrees. Eight eighths of the sky covered by low clouds. Type of low clouds, stratus or fractostratus, but not fractostratus of the type usually associated with bad weather. Height of cloud layer 300 to 600 feet. Direction of ship, eastward at 10 to 12 knots. The barometer has been falling then steady with a net change of -2.0 millibars during the past three hours. Sea temperature 6 degrees warmer

than the air. Dew point temperature 40 degrees. Direction of waves indeterminate.

This code has been in use since January 1, 1949, and is known as the Washington Synoptic Code. Because of mutual understanding among nations through the WMO, this numerical code of seven groups consisting of five figures each can be decoded by thousands of collecting centers throughout the world.

The collecting centers to which the *Irish Oak* and other ships report depends upon their location. The Commission for Maritime Meteorology has constructed world areas for shipping forecasts. These not only designate the centers to which ships report but indicate the range of forecasting areas for which individual WMO members are responsible.

The *Irish Oak,* for example, is at present on the North Atlantic run. Her officers will direct their reports to "Observer Washington" when West of 40W. and to "Weatherdun Wire London" when East of 40W. The messages of the *Irish Oak* may be received at any of several coast radio stations in the New England area. Her reports are then relayed to the Weather Bureau Communications Center at Washington, D.C., either by commercial telegraph circuits or by special teletypewriter line.

At the Weather Bureau Communications Center, hundreds of such reports are being received from ships at sea. Along with these are 750 others from weather stations in North America and the West Indies, plus 2,000 more from stations in Europe, Asia, North Africa, and northern South America. From this weather picture taken by almost 3,000 pairs of eyes, the Synoptic Reports and Forecasts Division of the Weather Bureau constructs reports of the weather situation around the hemisphere.

These reports are then transmitted throughout the WMO area of responsibility for the United States. Bulletins containing North American weather data are broadcast by Radio Stations WSY, New York, and WEK, New Orleans, to other meteorological services throughout the world. Some 70 low-power government and commercial shore radio stations broadcast at least twice daily bulletins to ships in coastal waters. Special weather bulletins for shipping in eastern North Pacific waters are made by Radio Stations KPH, Bolinas, and KTK, San Francisco, California. Similar bulletin broadcasts for shipping in western North Atlantic waters are broadcast by Radio Station NSS, Washington, D.C. It is from this latter station that the radio operator aboard the *Irish Oak* receives the marine forecasts, storm warnings, and reports for which his ship had been partially responsible.

If problems arise in regard to weather observations and reports on shipboard the director of one of the meteorological services may refer the matter to the President of the Commission for Maritime Meteorology, WMO. Technical experts in the working groups of this Commission study such reports and make recommendations to member nations through the WMO. Sessions of this Commission are constantly striving to improve the collecting, coordination, and distribution of data in the field of maritime meteorology.

The Ship Reporting Program of the Commission for Maritime Meteorology is a practical example of the way in which the neighborhoods of the world may help themselves by helping one another. The WMO weather workshop forecasts an impressive way toward world peace.

Mr. I. R. Tannehill of the United States Weather Bureau, a member of the Commission for Synoptic Meteorology, WMO, has described the significance of this intergovernmental cooperation in the following words:

The weather is not influenced by national boundaries. It is true in many countires that the people are much more concerned with the weather which originates in other countries than with that which originates in their own country. Hurricanes pass over or near to the countries of the Caribbean area. They may devastate sections of the United States. A storm off the coast of France may be of little concern, but subsequently it may develop and be destructive in the Netherlands. Dust storms of Africa sometimes invade southern Italy. Cold waves from Canada cause misery and sometimes loss of life and property in the United States. Typhoons in the Philippines strike China and Japan. The bitterly cold weather of Central Europe comes from European Russia. It is obvious that the exchange of weather information is absolutely necessary. This requires world uniformity, and an efficient universal means of communication, that is, a weather language which is understood equally well in every country in the world. Surface ships and aircraft of all countries need to know about the weather in other parts of the world, across national boundaries and beyond continental and oceanic limitations.

WORLD METEOROLOGICAL ORGANIZATION: WMO

International Headquarters:
Avenue de la Paix, Geneva, Switzerland

Origin

International cooperation in meteorology had its beginnings in Brussels, Belgium, in 1853, when representatives from ten nations met to work out a program for collecting certain meteorological observations made at sea. This meeting was inspired by Matthew Fontaine Maury (1806-1873) of the United States Navy.

Matthew Maury had become lame through an accident in 1839. As a result, the Navy Department had relieved him of duties with the fleet and in 1841 had put him in charge of Navy charts and instruments. Out of this responsibility Commander Maury developed an organization from which grew the naval observatory and the hydrographic office. Matthew Maury sensed the importance of international cooperation in maritime meteorology. Commenting upon what was probably one of the first international scientific conferences ever held, Maury later wrote: "The Conference, having brought to a close its labors with respect to the facts to be collected, and the means to be employed for that purpose, has now only to express a hope that whatever observations may be made will be turned to useful account when received and not be suffered to lie dormant for want of a department to discuss them."

Commander Maury's hopes were to be realized. Other meetings followed and at Leipzig, Germany, in 1872 the International Meteorological Organization was formed. The International Meteorological Organization made many constructive contributions to the techniques and standardization of meteorological reporting. However, rapid developments in aviation and marine navigation gave rise to new and complicated problems in applied meteorology. In addition, meteorology was becoming increasingly important to the proper functioning of other activities, such as international telecommunications.

The Directors of the International Meteorological Organization, having cognizance of these developments through long years of experience, felt that their organization should be strengthened by becoming intergovernmental. A most natural second step would be an affiliation with the United Nations as a Specialized Agency for efficient and close cooperation with other international organizations. As a result, the Directors drew up the terms for the Convention of the World Meteorological Organization, WMO, at Washington, D.C., in 1947.

The Convention of the WMO became effective on March 23, 1950, thirty days after the thirtieth government had ratified its provisions. The functions, activities, assets, and obligations of the International Meteorological Organization were transferred to WMO. The First Congress of the WMO met at Paris on March 19, 1951. A United Nations-World Meteorological Organization Agreement was approved by the UN General Assembly on December 20, 1951.

Purpose and Functions

Article 2 of the WMO Convention states the purpose and functions of the Organization as follows:

a. To facilitate world-wide cooperation in the establishment of networks of stations for the making of meteorological observations or other geophysical observations related to meteorology and to promote the establishment and maintenance of meteorological centers charged with the provision of meteorological services;

b. To promote the establishment and maintenance of systems for the rapid exchange of weather information;

c. To promote standardization of meteorological observations and to ensure the uniform publication of observations and statistics;

d. To further the application of meteorology to aviation, shipping, agriculture, and other human activities; and

e. To encourage research and training in meteorology and to assist in coordinating the international aspects of such research and training.

Membership

As of May 1, 1954, WMO had eighty-two members. A complete listing of these members appears in the Appendix.

Structure and Organization

The constituent bodies of the WMO are the Congress, the Executive Committee, the Regional Associations, the Technical Commissions, and the Secretariat.

CONGRESS

The governing body of the Organization is the Congress. Members of the WMO Congress are the heads of the meteorological services in their respective countries or territories. The Congress is convened at least every four years. As the policy-making body, the Congress adopts technical regulations on meteorological practices and procedures, establishes financial and staff regulations, and elects the Secretary-General.

EXECUTIVE COMMITTEE

The Executive Committee is composed of fifteen members, including the three officers (President and two Vice-Presidents) of the Organization, the Presidents of the Six Regional Associations, and six Directors of meteorological services of member states or territories who are elected by the Congress. This body meets annually to carry out the policies of the Congress.

REGIONAL ASSOCIATIONS

The WMO Congress established six Regional Associations composed of member states and territories whose meteorological networks lie in or extend into one of these areas. The regions are Africa, Asia, South America, North and Central America, the Southwest Pacific, and Europe. Regional Associations meet as often as is necessary to comply with WMO policy. They coordinate meteorological and associated activities in their own regions and make recommendations to the Congress and the Executive Committee.

TECHNICAL COMMISSIONS

Eight Technical Commissions have been established by the Congress. They are composed of technical experts in their respective fields of pure and applied meteorology. They advise other international organizations on meteorological questions, make recommendations to the Congress and Executive Committee, and maintain close touch with one another through the WMO Secretariat. Technical Commissions are established in the following fields: aerology, aeronautical meteorology, agricultural meteorology, bibliography and publications, olimatology, instruments and methods of observation, maritime meteorology, and synoptic meteorology.

SECRETARIAT

The Secretariat consists of two divisions, one administrative and the other technical. The Secretariat serves as the administrative, documentary, and informational center for the WMO. Approved WMO publications are processed by the Secretariat. Studies of technical importance to WMO are made by staff experts in the offices in Geneva.

Activities

The following activities of Technical Commissions are illustrative of the scope of WMO's work: Aerology, working with the International Radio Consultative Committee of ITU on data with regard to thunderstorm influences on background noise-level at different frequencies; Aeronautical Meteorology, preparing an observing manual for aircrews; Agricultural Meteorology, studying the meteorological aspects of arid-zone research problems; Bibliography and Publications; preparing an International Journal of Meteorology.

WMO is participating in the United Nations Expanded Program of Technical Assistance for Economic Development of Underdeveloped Countries (*Chapter* 13). WMO has sent an expert to Yugo-

Weather reports are distributed to Weather Bureau offices by teletypewriter circuits. Photo shows reports being entered on circuits at a communication center.

Pilots being briefed before takoff as to weather conditions forecast over route.

Flag signalling in international code from a weather ship. In foreground a crewman telescopes a radio antenna.

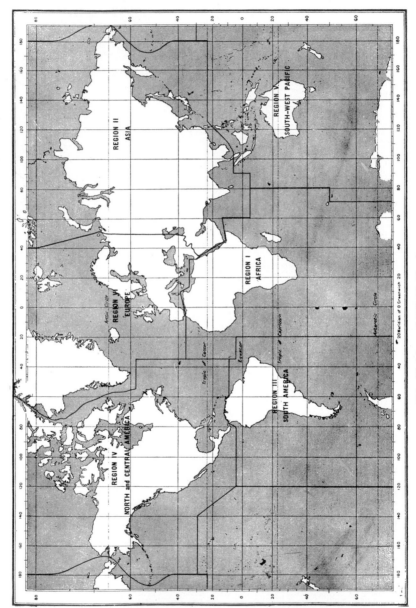

World Map of WMO Regions.

slavia upon that government's request for a survey of its meteorological facilities. The government of Libya requested WMO to draft a plan for the gradual establishment of a national meteorological service for that country. WMO will continue technical assistance by sending out missions and experienced technical personnel, by establishing research and training centers, and by providing scholarships and fellowships.

For many years nations have found it to their advantage to collaborate on meteorological matters. With the establishment of an intergovernmental workshop to further the application of meteorology to human activities, the neighborhoods of the world can anticipate safer transportation, better communications, and improved control over their agriculture, water resources, and health.

11

IRO

THE ROLAVS OF SKOOKUM BAY

*International Refugee Organization
1947-1952*

WHEN THE PREPARATORY COMMISSION of the International Refugee Organization began operations in 1947 it took over more than 700 displaced persons' camps. In these camps were approximately 1,200,000 people.

One of these camps was at Esslingen, Germany. Two of the many people living in this camp were Mr. and Mrs. Alfreds Rolavs. Their story is one of personal courage, good will among peoples, and the cooperation of a Specialized Agency of the United Nations.

The Rolavs grew up in the little town of Liepaja, Latvia. Liepaja is a fishing village, and it was only natural that Alfreds would follow the village tradition and earn his living from the catch in the Baltic Sea. Marija went to work in the village creamery after she finished school and it was there that she met Alfreds.

They were married in 1939, shortly before the outbreak of World War II. The years that had promised so much gave so little. Alfreds had purchased a farm on the outskirts of the village, and there they hoped to find security despite the war. But in 1944 the German Army moved into Liepaja, and in that same year Alfreds and Marija were shipped west into Germany for forced labor.

At their jobs in a creamery near Danzig, the days dragged by, one more monotonous than the next. Then came the confusion following liberation. The Rolavs sought refuge in a displaced persons' camp at Esslingen in the United States Occupation Zone of Germany. At

138

this time the camp was being operated by the United Nations Relief and Rehabilitation Administration.

When the IRO took over the DP camp at Esslingen, the Rolavs, along with all other refugees, were interviewed to establish their right to assistance under the IRO Constitution. Refugees were required to furnish valid reasons for not returning to their country of origin and to prove that they were not firmly established in Germany. While IRO gave assistance to those persons wishing to return to their homeland, the Constitution specifically stated that no refugee would be required to go anywhere against his will.

After the Rolavs had been admitted to IRO assistance services, they went through a series of steps designed to prepare them for resettlement. These included vocational tests for occupational skills, language-training courses, films and lectures to acquaint them with conditions of life in the various countries willing to accept refugees, and finally a chance to state their preference as to the land in which they wished to resettle. The Rolavs made the United States their choice.

But in 1947 the quotas for admission to the United States were quite small. At the time, the quotas of the immigration laws of 1921 and 1924 were in effect. Although the President had directed that refugees and displaced persons in the United States Zones of Germany and Austria were to be given preferences under the existing quotas, just 236 Latvians could be admitted in any one year.

The Rolavs knew through the information lectures at the camp that this situation existed, but they had so set their hearts on coming to the United States that they refused to make another choice and determined to make the best of their situation. Marija enrolled in a vocational course in needlework. Alfreds went to work each day as a laborer for the United States Army. They entered into the social and recreational life of the camp. This was the routine of their lives through 1947 and 1948.

In the latter year, events were taking place in the United States that brightened the hopes the Rolavs held. On June 25, 1948, the Congress adopted the Displaced Persons Act. This Act provided for the admission of 205,000 displaced persons and refugees. The Act was later amended to allow for the immigration of 313,000 refugees and displaced persons living temporarily in Germany, Austria, and Italy. Special legislation created a Displaced Persons Commission to carry out the provisions of the Act, with the IRO serving as an executive agent with the help of recognized voluntary societies in the United States.

One of the voluntary societies that worked closely with the IRO was the National Lutheran Council. Miss Lillian Franzen was the Lutheran Resettlement Service Executive in the state of Washington, and she was very active in publicizing and implementing the IRO resettlement program. Part of her work was to obtain assurances of jobs and housing for qualified refugees from residents of Washington.

Out on Little Skookum Bay near Shelton, Washington, Mr. Frank Bishop had a clam and oyster business and he needed someone to help him run it. Moreover, he had a plot of land that would make an ideal place on which to build a house for his employee. Learning of the National Lutheran Council program, Mr. Bishop indicated his willingness to accept a suitable couple under the IRO resettlement program. Mr. Bishop's offer of employment and housing was known as an "undesignated" assurance, in contrast to a "nominated" assurance. Nominated assurances were those in which the sponsor had a particular family in mind, while undesignated assurances were left to be filled by the voluntary society's representative overseas.

In order to lend assistance to the Lutheran World Federation in filling undesignated assurances, Miss Franzen interviewed refugees who had already settled in Washington to obtain their recommendations for people still in camps. It was at the suggestion of Mr.

Richard Deksenieks, the first DP to be settled in Washington state, that the Rolavs were proposed for an undesignated assurance.

The National Lutheran Council submitted Mr. Bishop's assurance, along with others, to the Displaced Persons Commission in Washington, D.C., and sent copies to the Lutheran World Federation. The Displaced Persons Commission approved Mr. Bishop's offer and sent notification of this action to their representatives in Frankfurt, Germany. The government representatives in Frankfurt advised the Lutheran World Federation that they might proceed.

The approved assurance was forwarded to the camp at Esslingen, and the Rolavs received the long-awaited word that they were to be sent to the resettlement center at Ludwigsburg. By 1949, IRO had established twenty resettlement centers where the selected refugees might be assembled for documentation, medical examination, and interview by representatives of the government willing to accept them.

These were days of anxiety for the Rolavs. After more than three years of hope, there was now the fear that something might go wrong at the last minute. But thanks to the friendly counsel of the Lutheran World Federation and their own personal qualifications they met each test at the resettlement center. The final interview with a United States Government official established their acceptance under the Displaced Persons Act.

The Rolavs were moved from Ludwigsburg to the IRO staging center of Camp Grohn in Bremen. The staging centers were used to gather at one assembly point all refugees who were ready to leave Europe after being accepted in one of the resettlement centers. This made it possible for the IRO to have an immediate quota of passengers when shipping facilities became available. While the refugees waited for transport, they had an opportunity to learn of procedures aboard ship and also to continue with their language courses.

From Camp Grohn the Rolavs moved to the IRO embarkation center at Bremerhaven. Here documents were checked, final immunization was administered, baggage labeled, and berths assigned. On the day of departure the Rolavs boarded the IRO-chartered ship the *General Sturgis*. On board ship the IRO had a three-member staff: an escort officer who, with an assistant, was responsible for the administration and well-being of the passengers, and a medical officer who supervised the health and sanitation program. These IRO employees were in addition to the ship's normal administrative and medical staffs.

The operations of the IRO fleet were controlled by the Central Shipping Office at international headquarters in Geneva. This office maintained daily contact with each vessel. These reports made it possible for the IRO to advise their representatives in ports of debarkation of arrival times and thus minimize difficulties of inland transport and housing.

The Rolavs arrived in Boston on November 26, 1949. Their ship was met at the pier by the IRO port liaison officer. After verifying the Rolavs' documents the IRO official turned their affairs over to representatives of the National Lutheran Council. Thus, for the first time in over two and a half years, the Rolavs ceased to be a part of the IRO.

During that time the Rolavs had shared in the vast care and maintenance program developed by IRO. At each living, resettlement, staging and embarkation center were to be found a complete range of activities associated with community life. In addition to the necessities of housing, food, and clothing, IRO provided schools for children and adults, medical and health facilities, social activities, and numerous welfare services.

IRO developed new procedures in encouraging governments to open resettlement opportunities and in selecting and processing refugees when opportunities became available. The orderly transport of refugees from living centers to the countries of immigration required new techniques of coordination. The entire resettlement program from the application for IRO assistance to settlement overseas gradually developed into a smoothly functioning scheme of working procedures.

However successful the IRO administration had been, the real measure of the worth of the program is to be found in the futures of the peoples who were resettled.

When the National Lutheran Council port and dock representatives met the Rolavs at the pier in Boston they assisted them through customs and arranged for their inland transportation and shipment of baggage. After the Rolavs had boarded the train that was to take them to Tacoma, Washington, the Boston representatives advised Miss Franzen of their travel arrangements so that they could be met upon arrival.

Also on hand to greet the Rolavs in Tacoma were Mr. and Mrs. Bishop. Together they returned to Lynch Road on Little Skookum Bay. Here the Rolavs were taken through the new cottage that had been built for them. For the first time in five years they had a home of their own!

From their new home the Rolavs created a new life. In less than six months they had repaid the National Lutheran Council the money that had been loaned for their trip across the continent. Alfreds contributed to the expansion of the Bishops' oyster and clam business. Nearby were old friends from the days at Esslingen camp, and new acquaintances were made through their interests in the church and other community activities.

The Rolavs have become respected members of their community. They take pride in their new homeland. Their happiness is a tribute to their courage, the generosity of the Bishops, the idealism of the National Lutheran Council, and the efficiency of the IRO. Working together, they have demonstrated that good neighbors in one part of the world can become good neighbors in another.

INTERNATIONAL REFUGEE ORGANIZATION: IRO

(July 1, 1947–January 31, 1952)

Origin

On February 12, 1946 the General Assembly of the United Nations passed by unanimous vote a resolution which recognized that the problem of refugees and displaced persons created by World War II was of immediate urgency. For the ten months that followed this resolution the approach to this problem was the subject of debate in the General Assembly, the Economic and Social Council, and in various committees established by the latter group. Finally, on December 15, 1946, the Constitution of the International Refugee Organization was adopted as part of a resolution passed by the General Assembly and was opened for ratification on the same date.

Concurrent with the adoption of the IRO Constitution, the Assembly established the machinery for a Preparatory Commission which was to function until such time as the IRO Constitution became operative. On July 1, 1947, this Preparatory Commission took over the refugee and displaced persons responsibilities of the United Nations Relief and Rehabilitation Administration along with those of the Intergovernmental Committee on Refugees. The Constitution of IRO came into effect on August 20, 1948; the Preparatory Commission functioned until the following September 16th.

Purpose

IRO's purpose was to solve the tragic human problem presented by the hundreds of thousands of persons uprooted by World War II. When the Preparatory Commission began operations it took over more than 700 Displaced Persons camps in Germany, Austria, Italy, the Middle East, Africa, and Asia. In these camps were approximately 1,200,000 persons.

Functions

To accomplish its task, IRO was confronted with the following tasks:

1. To care for the refugees and rehabilitate those requiring such help to enable them to support themselves;
2. To repatriate those who wanted to return to their former homes;
3. To find opportunities in other countries for those who wanted to emigrate, and to transport them to those countries; and
4. To make the best arrangements possible for the local settlement of those who either could not resettle or who preferred to remain where they were.

Membership

Eighteen nations ratified the IRO Constitution and contributed funds to augment its purpose. Australia, Belgium, Canada, China, Denmark, the Dominican Republic, France, Guatemala, Iceland, Italy, Luxembourg, the Netherlands, New Zealand, Norway, Switzerland, the United Kingdom, the United States, and Venezuela participated in this world-wide humanitarian enterprise.

Structure and Organization

The policy-making body of IRO was the General Council in which each member had one representative and one vote. An Executive Committee of nine members carried out the policies established by the General Council. In addition a Review Board of Eligibility Appeals, consisting of three persons (who served as individuals) made decisions in particular cases of eligibility of refugees and displaced persons.

Activities

At the height of its activity, IRO had under charter a migration fleet of thirty-six vessels; its international personnel numbered more than two thousand and its annual budget of $155,000,000 was more than that of the United Nations and all the Specialized Agencies combined.

The total budget of IRO for its approximate four-year operation was $412,691,915. Approximately 1,045,000 Displaced Persons were re-established in new homes and about 73,000 returned to their former homelands. Well over 1,600,000 persons received some form of IRO assistance.

Mr. J. Donald Kingsley, Director-General of IRO, summarized his opinions of this workshop for the world in a statement at Geneva on January 4, 1952:

> Never before in history had such a problem been tackled by the international community and never before, I believe, was any problem so humanely, democratically, and expeditiously dealt with. The results achieved stand as a lasting tribute to the democratic world.

SHIPS AT SEA

*Inter-Governmental Maritime
Consultative Organization*

A Specialized Agency in the Making

FOR MANY YEARS private individuals and government officials have sensed the need for an intergovernmental organization that would concern itself with problems in ocean shipping and ocean travel.

Many economic as well as technical problems connected with ocean transport have been cumbersome of solution because no competent organization has had authority to deal with them. These concerned the rendering of assistance to vessels in distress, determination of legal responsibility in case of collision, salvage of shipwrecked cargoes, rules of the road, international signals, standardization of tonnage measurements, safety regulations, rights of foreign vessels in ports of other nations, and the right of inland nations to possess ocean fleets.

With the coming into being of the United Nations the consideration of this problem fell to the Economic and Social Council. The Council at its meeting at London in 1946 adopted a resolution creating a Temporary Transport and Communications Commission. This Commission was to advise the Council on the problems involved in the general field of international transport and communications, and to survey the international organizations then operating in this area.

In May 1946 the newly created Temporary Transport and Communications Commission met at New York and drafted a report that included, among other items, a listing of intergovernmental bodies in the shipping field. There were just three such standing organizations: the United Maritime Consultative Council, the International Hydrographic Bureau, and the International Commission for the Maintenance of the Lighthouse at Cape Spartel. The first of these was a temporary organization that grew out of the need for the co-ordination of shipping during World War II and the immediate postwar period. The International Hydrographic Bureau had been organized in 1921 for the purpose of sharing information on ocean surveys, measuring instruments, and charts. The International Commission of the Cape Spartel Light was established in 1865 under a treaty approved by eleven nations, including the United States, for the purpose of guaranteeing the management, maintenance, and permanent neutrality of the Cape Spartel Light located on the African side of the approaches to the Straits of Gibraltar.

In view of the limited number of international organizations in the field of shipping, the Temporary Commission recommended that the Economic and Social Council should take the initiative in setting up an intergovernmental body to deal with the over-all problems in this field. Acting upon this recommendation, a committee of the Economic and Social Council requested the Secretary-General of the United Nations to ask the opinion of the United Maritime Consultative Council on this matter. Underscoring the importance of this need, the Economic and Social Council in June 1946 established a permanent Transport and Communications Commission.

The final session of the United Maritime Consultative Council held in October 1946 adopted four recommendations: that an Inter-Governmental Consultative Organization should be established as a Specialized Agency of the United Nations; that member governments should request the Economic and Social Council to convene a conference for this purpose; that a Provisional Maritime Consultative

Council should be established; and that member governments be encouraged to join the latter organization. Annexed to the recommendations of the United Maritime Consultative Council was a draft agreement for an intergovernmental maritime consultative organization.

The Transport and Communications Commission began its first session at New York on February 6, 1947. It recommended that the Economic and Social Council invite interested governments to participate in a United Nations Maritime Conference. This conference met at Geneva on February 19, 1946. Representatives of thirty-two governments participated, with observers present from four additional governments. Dr. J. J. Oyevaar of the Netherlands was chosen President of the Conference.

It was quickly determined that the three basic questions that must be resolved at the Conference were the following:

1. Should a separate maritime organization be established?

2. Should the organization's activities include both technical and economic affairs?

3. How should the organizational structure be established so as to balance the interests of the ship-providing and ship-using nations?

Australia and New Zealand proposed that shipping problems should be handled through a commission of the United Nations rather than in a new intergovernmental organization. The reply to this proposal was made by Sir Ramaswami Mudaliar of India, a former chairman of the Economic and Social Council. His contention was that the United Nations commissions were not set up to deal with the carrying out of long-range functions in the field of shipping, and that a Specialized Agency was the answer to the problem. This proposal carried the Conference, and the first basic question was resolved.

The second question, that of limiting the activities of the proposed organization, was debated at length. Article I of the Convention (included in this chapter) contains important compromises resulting from these discussions. The Scandinavian countries and Finland opposed these compromises.

Debate on the third question centered about the allocation of representatives to the Council of the Organization. The formula for distribution of membership was the occasion for a great deal of controversy, and eventually led to the formal withdrawal of Panama from the Conference.

The Convention was finally hammered into shape. In the final vote cast on March 6, 1948, twenty-one nations approved the document, one opposed, seven abstained, and three were absent. Considering the divergence of the national views, the Conference was a successful one. Not only was there a sincere desire to establish an intergovernmental body to consider shipping problems, but there also existed a spirit of compromise that in the long run reconciled the different points of view.

The Secretary-General of the United Nations was authorized by the Convention to receive instruments of acceptance from those nations desiring to join IMCO. The Organization will be established when its Constitution has been ratified by twenty-one states, of which seven shall have at least one million gross tons of shipping. As of January 1954, fourteen governments—Argentina, Australia, Belgium, Burma, Canada, Dominican Republic, France, Greece, Haiti, Ireland, Israel, the Netherlands, the United Kingdom, and the United States —had ratified the Convention. Of this group, eight have a total tonnage of not less than one million gross tons of shipping, so that ratification depends upon acceptance by eight additional governments.

During the five years since the Geneva Conference, the Transport and Communications Commission has initiated numerous inquiries to governments through the Secretary-General requesting the status of ratification proceedings. The Commission has advised the governments concerned that many urgent and pressing problems are dependent upon the establishment of IMCO. Many other international organizations are hampered in their work by the fact that there is no organization available for consultation on the maritime aspects of mutual problems.

IMCO will complete the group of international organizations that the United Nations considers important in coordinating technical and economic problems of transport and communication. Together with the International Civil Aviation Organization, the International Telecommunication Union, and the World Meteorological Organization, IMCO will complete a well-balanced team of intergovernmental organizations competent to deal with world-wide problems of great importance.

INTER-GOVERNMENTAL MARITIME CONSULTATIVE ORGANIZATION: IMCO

The IMCO Convention will enter into force on the date when twenty-one states, of which seven must have at least one million gross tons of shipping, have deposited instruments of ratification with the Secretary-General of the United Nations.

International Headquarters: London, England

Purposes

IMCO's purposes are established in Part I of the Convention.

Article 1

a. to provide machinery for cooperation among Governments in the field of governmental regulation and practices relating to technical matters of all kinds affecting shipping engaged in international trade, and to encourage the general adoption of the highest practicable standards in matters concerning maritime safety and efficiency of navigation;

b. to encourage the removal of discriminatory action and unnecessary restrictions by Governments affecting shipping engaged in international trade so as to promote the availability of shipping services to the commerce of the world without discrimination; assistance and encouragement given by a Government for the development of its national shipping and for purposes of security does not in itself constitute discrimination, provided that such assistance and encouragement is not based on measures designed to restrict the freedom of shipping of all flags to take part in international trade;

c. to provide for the consideration by the Organization of matters concerning unfair restrictive practices by shipping concerns in accordance with Part II;

d. to provide for the consideration by the Organization of matters concerning unfair restrictive practices by shipping concerns in accordance with Part II;

e. to provide for the exchange of information among Governments on matters under consideration by the Organization.

Functions

IMCO's functions are established in Part II of the Convention.

Article 2

The functions of the Organization shall be consultative and advisory.

velve-year-old Dace Epermanis (holding
wers) gets a special send-off at Bremerhaven,
rmany, when records of the IRO disclosed
t she was the 150,000th person to be ad-
tted to the U. S. A. under its Displaced Per-
s law.

Mr. Rolavs contributes to the expansion of the
Bishops' oyster and clam business.

e of the refugees from IRO camps in Ger-
y, Austria and Italy are shown boarding an
-chartered ship at Bremerhaven for the
. A.

Mr. and Mrs. Alfreds Rolavs of Skookum Bay.

The officers of the United Nations Transport and Communications Commission: Mr. Willem L. De Vries (left) of the Netherlands, Chairman; and Sir H. Osborne Mance of the United Kingdom, Vice-Chairman.

The Government of Burma formally becomes a party to the convention of the Intergovernmental Maritime Consultative Organization. Mr. James Barrington (right), Representative of Burma, presents that country's acceptance to Mr. A. H. Feller, formerly Principal Director of the United Nations Legal Department.

France ratifies the IMCO Convention at United Nations Headquarters. Mr. Philippe de Seynes (left) presents the instrument of ratification to Mr. Ivan S. Kerno, Assistant Secretary-General in charge of the Legal Department.

Article 3

In order to achieve the purposes set out in Part I, the functions of the Organization shall be:

a. subject to the provisions of Article 4, to consider and make recommendations upon matters arising under Article 1 (*a.*), (*b.*) and (*c.*) that may be remitted to it by Members, by any organ or Specialized Agency of the United Nations or by any other intergovernmental organization or upon matters referred to it under Article 1 (*d.*)

b. to provide for the drafting of conventions, agreements, or other suitable instruments, and to recommend these to Governments and to intergovernmental organizations, and to convene such conferences as may be necessary;

c. to provide machinery for consultation among Members and the exchange of information among Governments.

Article 4

In those matters which appear to the Organization capable of settlement through the normal processes of international shipping business the Organization shall so recommend. When, in the opinion of the Organization, any matter concerning unfair restrictive practices by shipping concerns is incapable of settlement through the normal processes of international shipping business, or has in fact so proved, and provided it shall first have been the subject of direct negotiations between the Members concerned, the Organization shall, at the request of one of those Members, consider the matter.

Membership

Members of the United Nations may become members of IMCO by depositing instruments of ratification. Other states may become members upon recommendation of the Council and approval by two-thirds of the members. Territories whose international affairs are the responsibility of a member or of the United Nations may become associate members through communication of this desire by the member or by the United Nations to the Secretary-General of the United Nations.

Structure and Organization

IMCO's Convention provides for an Assembly, a Council, a Maritime Safety Committee, and a Secretariat.

ASSEMBLY

The Assembly consists of all members and meets every two years. The Assembly elects four members of the Council and the members of the Maritime Safety Committee. It considers and reviews reports of the Council and votes the budget of the Organization. The Assembly recommends to members for adoption regulations concerning maritime safety which have been referred to it by the Maritime Safety Committee through the Council.

COUNCIL

The Council consists of sixteen members: six represent governments with the largest interest in providing international shipping services, six represent other governments with the largest interest in seaborne trade, and four are elected by the Assembly from governments having a substantial interest in providing international shipping services, or in international seaborne trade.

The Council meets as often as necessary to discharge its responsibilities. The Council receives reports from the Maritime Safety Committee and transmits them to the Assembly. The Council submits reports to the Assembly reviewing IMCO's activities between Assembly sessions. It submits budget estimates, with recommendations, to the Assembly. The Council appoints the Secretary-General with the approval of the Assembly and makes provisions for staff appointments and conditions of employment.

MARITIME SAFETY COMMITTEE

The Maritime Safety Committee consists of fourteen members elected by the Assembly from among nations with an important interest in maritime safety. No fewer than eight members shall represent the largest ship-owning nations. Members are elected for a term of four years and may be eligible for re-election. The Committee meets regularly once a year, and at other times upon the request of five members.

The Committee considers such matters as aids to navigation, construction and equipment of vessels, rules for the prevention of collisions, the handling of dangerous cargoes, and other matters. The Committee may perform whatever duties are assigned it by the Assembly. The Committee is charged with maintaining close relationships with other intergovernmental bodies concerned with transport and communication in promoting maritime safety and rescue.

SECRETARIAT

The Secretariat includes the Secretary-General, a Secretary of the Maritime Safety Committee, and such staff as the Council may determine necessary for the proper administration of the Organization.

Activities

The activities of the Organization will include many now performed by other international groups. A convention approved by the International Safety of Life at Sea Conference in 1948 and subsequently ratified by thirty-seven nations established the call "S O S" as the international distress signal. This call became officially operative on January 1, 1954. It may be assumed that actions of this kind will fall to IMCO when its Convention is ratified.

13 | TEAMWORK

The United Nations Technical Assistance Board

Coordinating the Work of the Specialized Agencies

THE UNITED NATIONS, under Article 55 of its Charter, is pledged to "promote higher standards of living, full employment, and conditions of economic progress and development." Responsibility for achieving this aim is charged to the Economic and Social Council that in turn is responsible to the General Assembly.

The collective aim of the Specialized Agencies might be summed up in much the same terms as those expressed in Article 55. However, it will be recalled that the activities of the Specialized Agencies are directed toward suggesting ways within their particular fields in which these goals might be achieved by their individual members. The necessity of coordinating the work that two or more Agencies might accomplish for a given area was recognized at an early date. For example, improving the health of a nation and thus reducing the mortality rate might not actually "promote a higher standard of living" if not accompanied by improved techniques in food production. Accordingly, an Administrative Committee on Coordination was established by the Economic and Social Council. This Committee is composed of the Secretary-General of the United Nations and the executive heads of the Specialized Agencies.

The work of the Agencies, however, remained limited by the size

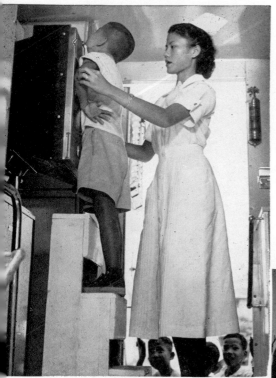

United Nations - WHO - UNICEF technical assistance to the Philippines includes anti-TB campaigns. A nurse inside a van presented by UNICEF prepares a boy for x-ray examination.

Under the United Nations Technical Assistance Program FAO helps Ethiopia in the fight against rinderpest, the disease that at one time killed a million head of cattle yearly. Dr. Frank Vandemael, of FAO, examines a cow for signs of rinderpest.

A UNESCO Technical Assistance Mission to Liberia trains skilled personnel needed for the country's developing economy. Dr. Henry C. McBay, of the United States, UNESCO teacher of chemistry, is shown explaining a problem to his class at Liberia College, Monrovia.

General view of a meeting of the Second Technical Assistance Conference held in Paris. Fifty-one countries pledged a total of $18,802,000 for operations of the United Nations Expanded Program of Technical Assistance.

Partial view of a meeting of the Economic and Social Council. Representatives of the Specialized Agencies are seated to the right.

of their budgets. In addition, there were some fields of importance to the realization of Article 55 with which no established Agency was equipped to deal. These included such areas as industrial development, inland transport, public finance, public administration, and social welfare.

With these considerations in mind the General Assembly of the United Nations, beginning in 1946, passed a series of resolutions providing for technical assistance to help meet the needs of the people of the underdeveloped countries for the technical knowledge and skills required to build up their economies.

The earliest program provided advisory social welfare services to requesting governments. Gradually the program was developed until in 1949 the General Assembly approved the creation of a comprehensive plan for an expanded program of technical assistance through the United Nations and the Specialized Agencies. This plan had been submitted to the Assembly by the Economic and Social Council and had been drafted by the Secretary-General of the United Nations and the heads of eight Specialized Agencies: ILO, FAO, UNESCO, ICAO, the International Bank, the International Monetary Fund, WHO and the IRO.

The Assembly when approving the program also established the Technical Assistance Board to coordinate the work of the program. The Board consists of representatives of the Food and Agriculture Organization, the World Health Organization, the International Labor Organization, UNESCO, the International Civil Aviation Organization, and the Technical Assistance Administration of the United Nations. The International Bank and the International Monetary Fund also cooperate in the work of the Board to coordinate their technical assistance activities with those under the Expanded Program, but they do not receive money from the Program's funds. In 1951 the International Telecommunication Union and the World Meteorological Organization became participants in the Program. At the present time these two organizations receive a portion of the funds earmarked for the Technical Assistance Administration.

The Board is responsible to the Technical Assistance Committee of the Economic and Social Council, which in turn is responsible to the General Assembly of the United Nations.

All governments which are members of the United Nations, ILO, FAO, UNESCO, ICAO, and WHO are invited to participate in the Technical Assistance Program. The participating governments contribute funds that make the Program possible. Contributions are voluntary and are deposited in a Special Account set up by the Secretary-General of the United Nations. These funds are separate from the general budgets of the United Nations and the Specialized Agencies.

The sum pledged for the first period—July 1950 to December 31, 1951—was slightly in excess of twenty million dollars, and was designated by fifty-five governments. At the end of this period, twelve of the governments had made no payments. The sum pledged for the second period, which extended through the calendar year 1952, was just under nineteen million dollars. This amount was pledged by sixty-four governments, but all pledges were not met. The sum recommended by the Technical Assistance Committee of ECOSOC for the third period of 1953 was twenty-five million dollars. The sixty-four nations that attended the Third Technical Assistance Conference in February 1953 pledged just under twenty-one million dollars. This was later augmented by the pledges of three other nations that brought the total for 1953 to $22,395,687. Of this amount, $18,939,010 had been received by the end of 1953. By December 1953 participating nations had pledged $24,204,522 for the 1954 program.

This lag between pledges and actual contributions has posed two very difficult problems for the Technical Assistance Board. The first revolves around advance planning for projects to be undertaken by the Board in any one fiscal year. Unless some way can be found within which a firm budget can be established, a system of priorities must be established. This in turn leads to a secondary problem centered about the relative merits of projects.

No program of assistance is considered without a well-planned request from the government concerned. This, in fact, has been one of the very constructive parts of the Program: it has required governments to go over their own needs with a fine-tooth comb before deciding upon specific requests for aid, which in turn has given governments in underdeveloped areas a more realistic grasp of their total economic and social needs.

Generally speaking, assistance is provided in four ways: the provision of experts, as in Dr. Lin's work with the fish-farming project in Haiti; provisions for having a country's experts travel abroad; equipment (limited to 25% of the total funds allotted for the project); and the establishment of seminars and training centers.

One of the very constructive services provided by the Program has been that of the work performed by the resident representatives of the Technical Assistance Board. These representatives are called upon to provide governments with help in setting up requests for their programs. They harmonize the work of the various Organizations in the field. They serve as liaison with other technical assistance organizations, such as the Colombo Plan of the United Kingdom and the Point Four Program of the United States.

Many of the projects listed in preceding chapters under the activities engaged in by individual Agencies have been carried out under the Expanded Technical Assistance Program. Since the programs engaged in by the Technical Assistance Administration are not as well known, a few examples may serve to indicate the scope of the Administration's work.

Governments have requested assistance in developing industrial projects in oil drilling, mining production, electric power, textiles, salt technology, and cost accounting methods. Transport and communications assistance has been requested in the field of road, rail, and inland transportation. In cooperation with the Fund, the TAA provided assistance in the fields of fiscal, financial, and monetary problems. Particular emphasis was given to requests for the improvement of public administration in twelve different countries during 1953. Governments are being assisted in the preparation of statistical surveys such as population censuses. House and town planning, and the use of new techniques in low-cost housing, were among the other services requested by governments in 1953.

The effectiveness of the work being coordinated by the Technical Assistance Board cannot be fully determined after four short years of operation. A program of this kind that operates in many countries with a budget of slightly more than $20,000,000 a year is not designed to produce immediate and spectacular results. The long range impact will be one that springs from the development of new horizons, new attitudes, and new possibilities for the peoples of the world.

Whatever difficulties the Program may have to face, no one can deny its unique characteristic of universality. Neighborhoods are sharing techniques. They are learning that important skills are not necessarily concentrated in industrialized areas. Nations have learned that they need have no fear of foreign domination when they request United Nations technical assistance. The Specialized Agencies have developed productive ways of working together. Neighborhoods have learned that there are peoples in other lands who are sympathetic toward their problems. There is about the Program a spirit of *team-work* that builds a brotherhood of man.

14 | THE UNITED STATES IN THE SPECIALIZED AGENCIES

FOLLOWING WORLD WAR II, there was a marked change in the foreign policy of the United States. This was in keeping with the nation's assumption of a leading role in international affairs. One result of this change has been our active participation in virtually every international organization in the postwar period.

The basic objective of this participation is to forward the nation's interest in world affairs. The national interests of the United States coincide to a great degree with those of other nations. As we strive toward our goals of peace, freedom, and security, we have joined together with other nations to achieve these goals through democratic participation in intergovernmental organizations. In no field of international activity has this cooperation shown more constructive results than those growing out of the conventions, treaties, and recommendations of the Specialized Agencies.

The United States is an active member of each of the Specialized Agencies. Our participation, first of all, requires authorization by Congress. This authorization has taken various forms. We participate in the International Civil Aviation Organization, the International Telecommunication Union, the World Meteorological Organization, and the International Labor Organization (revised Constitution) under the regular treaty-making provisions of the Constitution of the United States. Our membership in the Food and Agriculture Organization, the World Health Organization, the International Refugee

Organization (1947-1951) and UNESCO is authorized by joint resolutions of Congress which have the effect of sanction for actions of the President. Our participation in the Fund, the Bank, and the Universal Postal Union is under the mandate of Acts of Congress.

The action taken by the government of the United States in the ratification of the Convention on the Maritime Consultative Organization (*Chapter* 12) serves as an example of general procedure.

The final document of the Conference of Geneva was signed for the United States by Mr. Garrison Norton and Mr. Huntington T. Morse of the U.S. delegation to this Conference on March 6, 1948. Mr. Norton, who headed the delegation, noted after his signature that his approval was "subject to acceptance" by his government.

On June 17, 1948, the Secretary of State transmitted a copy of the Convention to the President for his consideration. In a covering letter, the Secretary of State outlined the historical background of the Convention and indicated that the Department of State supported the document with the concurrence of the Department of Commerce, the United States Coast Guard, and the United States Maritime Commission. The Secretary further advised the President that representatives of the National Federation of American Shipping and of the Shipbuilders Council of America had been members of the U.S. delegation to the Conference, and that they too concurred in acceptance.

The Secretary of State further suggested a reservation in regard to the Convention. Article 4 of the IMCO Convention relates to the making of recommendations by the Organization in matters relating to unfair restrictive practices by shipping concerns. As alleged practices of this kind come under the review of the antitrust laws of the United States, the Secretary suggested the Senate insure that if the treaty were ratified it would not have the effect of altering the antitrust laws.

On June 18, 1948, the President transmitted the Convention to the Senate of the United States for its advice and consent, as required in Section 2, Article II, of the Constitution of the United States. The President recommended approval of the Convention with the reservation described by the Secretary of State.

The Convention was referred to the Committee on Foreign Relations in the Senate. Hearings were held on the Convention. Following approval by the Committee, its Chairman transmitted a report to the Senate urging advice and consent to the ratification of the Convention subject to the reservation and understanding suggested by the President. On June 27, 1950, the Senate ratified this treaty and in a joint resolution set forth its reservations.

The Convention was signed by the President and transmitted by the Department of State to the United States Representative to the United Nations. On August 21, 1950, Ambassador Warren R. Austin transmitted the instrument of ratification to the Secretary-General of the United Nations. In his letter of transmittal, Ambassador Austin conveyed the text of the Senate reservation and added that the statement was "merely a clarification of the intended meaning of the Convention and a safeguard against any possible misinterpretation."

Upon authorization by Congress, and the coming into existence of a Specialized Agency, the major responsibility for our participation falls to the Department of State. There are some Agencies, however, in which the Department of State does not assume primary responsibility, and these exceptions are worth noting.

United States relations with the Universal Postal Union and the World Meteorological Organization are the responsibility of the Post Office Department and the Department of Commerce through the United States Weather Bureau. Our relations with the Fund and the Bank are authorized by the Bretton Woods Agreements Act, which establishes a National Advisory Council on International Monetary and Financial Problems to advise the President on major problems arising out of the administration of these two Specialized Agencies.

This Council consists of the Secretary of Treasury (Chairman), the Secretary of State, the Secretary of Commerce, the Chairman of the Board of Governors of the Federal Reserve System, the Chairman of the Board of Directors of the Export-Import Bank of Washington, and, during such period as the Mutual Security Agency shall continue to exist, the Director for Mutual Security.

The official channel between the United States and the Specialized Agencies, other than those mentioned above, is the Bureau of United Nations Affairs in the Department of State. Within this Bureau the Office of United Nations Economic and Social Affairs is responsible for the development of United States policies and activities within the Agencies. This Office insures that spokesmen for United States policies follow a pattern that will not conflict with policies in other international organizations, and that the policy will represent the best possible judgment.

The Office of International Administration and Conferences handles the Bureau's many administrative problems arising from assembling and instructing delegates to international conferences. Two other offices in this Bureau concentrate on affairs directly related to United States participation in the General Assembly, Security Council, and Trusteeship Council of the United Nations.

The Bureau is headed by the Assistant Secretary for United Nations Affairs, who is directly responsible to the Under Secretary of State and through him to the Secretary of State. He gives approval to policies prepared by the various Offices within the Bureau, which are in turn transmitted to United States representatives at conferences of the Specialized Agencies. The Secretary conducts relations with other government agencies interested in Agency affairs, such as the Committee on the Food and Agriculture Organization (*Chapter* 1).

The Assistant Secretary also maintains close relations with the Congress through hearings before Congressional Committees and in meetings with subcomittees of the Senate Foreign Relations Com-

r. Edward P. Warner (right), President of the Council of ICAO,
shown explaining an illustrated display of aerodromes and aero-
rome equipment.

Mr. C. P. Vasudevan of India (left)
is studying all aspects of long dis-
tance and trunk telephone systems
with the American Telephone and
Telegraph Company in New York
City under the United Nations
Technical Assistance Fellowship
Program.

Mr. Montgomery Blair (1813-1883) who as Postmaster General of the United States was responsible for the first international postal conference in 1863.

Dr. F. W. Reichelderfer, President the World Meteorological Organizati (WMO) and Chief of the United Sta Weather Bureau.

Mr. Eugene R. Black, President International Bank for Reconstruction and Development.

Dr. Luther Evans, Director-G UNESCO.

mittee. These meetings not only serve the purpose of keeping the Congress posted on State Department activity in the Specialized Agencies, and other United Nations affairs, but they are also important in implementing decisions made by the Agencies that must at all times receive government approval before they become operative in the United States.

Public organizations, groups, and individuals communicate their opinions regarding United States participation in the Specialized Agencies, and other international organs, to the Department of State through the Division of Public Liaison in the Office of Public Affairs. This Division in turn may, upon the request of organizations or of the Bureau for United Nations Affairs, invite public groups to participate as consultants in policy matters.

The interest of public groups is of vital concern in the cause of international cooperation. The National Citizens' Committee for the World Health Organization may be cited as one of the many examples of organized public interest in Specialized Agency matters. This Committee held its first conference in Washington, D.C., in April 1953. Its purpose is to acquaint the American public with the relationship of public health to the general welfare and peace of the entire world, and to underscore the importance of international health programs.

American citizens are directly influencing the course of Specialized Agency affairs through the high offices they hold in the Organizations. These individuals are carrying on the American tradition of international cooperation and good will as it was established by such figures as Postmaster General Blair, Samuel Gompers, and Matthew Maury.

Dr. Francis W. Reichelderfer, Chief of the United States Weather Bureau, who has long been active in international meteorological organizations, was named the first President of the World Meteorological Organization in 1951. Dr. Edward Pearson Warner dates his first active participation in aviation back to 1910 when, at the age of sixteen, he entered a glider he had built himself in a meet sponsored by the Intercollegiate Aviation Society. His career since that date has touched virtually every phase of aviation, and was climaxed in May 1947, when the first Council of the International Civil Aviation Organization chose Dr. Warner as its new President—a position which he now holds. Mr. Eugene R. Black, President of the International Bank for Reconstruction and Development, was formerly senior Vice-President of the Chase National Bank, and has enjoyed a distinguished career in banking.

Dr. Philip V. Cardon, present Director-General of the Food and Agriculture Organization, knows farming from the ground up—a long way up, to national and international movements that bridge the gap between surplus and need. The administrative talents of David A. Morse were referred to in Chapter 5. On June 16, 1953, the Executive Board of the United Nations Educational, Scientific and Cultural Organization nominated Dr. Luther Evans, Librarian of Congress, for the post of Director-General. This nomination was approved by the UNESCO Conference.

Standing behind these leaders are hundreds of government officials who are contributing to the work of the Agencies. The World Meteorological Organization, for example, includes twenty United States government officials among the members of its various Commissions. Hundreds more of our citizens are members of the international civil service, contributing their talents to the effective operation of individual Agencies in dozens of varying capacities.

Individual citizens are contributing to the Agencies in many constructive ways. Private citizens have served as delegates to international conferences called by the Agencies. Others are serving on national commissions and organizations dedicated to furthering public interest in the Organizations. A $98,000,000 International Bank bond issue was completely sold in the United States during one day in January 1954. Local groups are underwriting UNESCO gift coupon sales, and other groups are increasing their knowledge of international affairs through studies of the Specialized Agencies.

A review of the purposes of the Specialized Agencies shows them to be democratic and humanitarian. These are ideals which Americans have demonstrated they are willing to support—so that the concept of democracy may be maintained, improved, and expanded throughout the neighborhoods of the world. The Specialized Agencies are workshops for the world—a world of peace, freedom, and friendship.

THE UNITED STATES IN THE SPECIALIZED AGENCIES

Food and Agriculture Organization: FAO

Authorization. The United States participates in FAO pursuant to a joint resolution approved July 31, 1945. On February 19, 1946, the President designated FAO as a public international organization entitled to enjoy the benefits of the International Organizations Immunities Act.

Payments. The United States contribution is paid from funds appropriated to the Department of State for this purpose. Its contribution for 1953 was $1,673,750.

Agencies Chiefly Concerned. The Departments of State, Agriculture, and Interior are primarily concerned with the work of FAO, but there is an Inter-Agency Committee, under the chairmanship of the Under Secretary of Agriculture, composed of representatives of the Departments of State, Agriculture, Interior, Commerce, Labor, Treasury, HEW (Health, Education and Welfare), and Bureau of the Budget, which advises the Secretary of State concerning United States policy in FAO and implementation of its recommendations.

Participation. The United States participates in sessions of the Conference by an offical voting member designated annually by the President, assisted by alternates and advisers. It participates officially in the Council through a member, alternate, and associate members designated by the President for each session.

International Civil Aviation Organization: ICAO

Authorization. The President ratified the Convention on International Civil Aviation on August 6, 1946, upon the advice and consent of the Senate. The instrument of ratification was deposited August 9, 1946. On May 31, 1947, the President designated the International Civil Aviation Organization as a public international organization entitled to enjoy the benefits of the International Organizations Immunities Act.

Payments. The United States contribution to ICAO is paid from funds appropriated to the Department of State for this purpose. The United States assessment for the calendar year 1953 was $815,112.

Agencies Chiefly Concerned. The agencies concerned are the Civil Aeronautics Board, the Civil Aeronautics Administration of the Department of Commerce, the Post Office Department, the Navy, the Air Force, and the Department of State. Coordination of U.S. participation in ICAO is handled through the Air Coordinating Committee.

Participation. The United States is the depository government for instruments of ratification of the ICAO treaty. The United States has been represented on the Council of ICAO since its beginning and in addition has representatives in Montreal specifically charged with representing this government on the Air Transport Committee and the Air Navigation Commission. The United

States maintains a permanent representative at the seat of ICAO in Montreal.

World Health Organization: WHO

Authorization. United States participation in WHO was authorized by a joint resolution approved by the President on June 14, 1948. On December 30, 1948, the President designated WHO as a public international organization entitled to enjoy the benefits of the International Organizations Immunities Act.

Payments. The United States pays its contribution out of funds appropriated to the Department of State for this purpose. Its contribution for the financial year 1953 was $2,866,667.

Agencies Chiefly Concerned. The Public Health Service of the Department of Health, Education and Welfare, and the Department of State are the United States agencies principally concerned with the United States participation in WHO.

Participation. The United States played a leading part in the movement that led to the establishment of WHO.

Universal Postal Union: UPU

Authorization. Authorization for the making of postal arrangements with foreign states rests currently upon the Act of June 12, 1934, which provides that the Postmaster General, by and with the advice and consent of the President, may negotiate and conclude postal treaties or conventions. The Universal Postal Convention of Paris of July 5, 1947, was signed by the Postmaster General, "by virtue of the powers vested by law in the Postmaster General, hereby ratified and approved, by and with the advice and consent of the President of the United States of America," on June 1, 1948; and the President approved the convention on June 9, 1948.

Payments. The United States contribution is paid from funds appropriated for the Post Office Department. Its contribution for 1953 was $13,911.

Agencies Chiefly Concerned. Delegates from the United States to the Universal Postal Congress are appointed by the Postmaster General.

Participation. The United States does not subscribe to the international parcel post, money order, c.o.d., and insurance services on the basis of Union agreements. Individual arrangements are made with each nation concerned, except in the case of the Parcel Post Agreement of the Postal Union of the Americas and Spain.

International Labor Organization: ILO

Authorization. By a joint resolution approved June 19, 1934, effective August 20, 1934, the Congress authorized the President on behalf of the United States to accept an invitation for membership in the International Labor Organization. The United States acceptance of the instrument of amendment of the ILO Constitution was deposited August 2, 1948, having been signed by the President pursuant to a joint resolution approved by Congress June 30, 1948. On February 19, 1946, the President designated the ILO as a public international organization entitled to enjoy the benefits of the International Organizations Immunities Act.

Payments. The United States contribution is paid from funds appropriated to the Department of State. The United States net assessment for 1953 was $1,538,991.

Agencies Chiefly Concerned. The determination of U.S. policy toward ILO is the responsibility of the Department of State. This responsibility is exercised in collaboration with the Department of Labor and other interested agencies of the Government.

Participation. Representatives of the Government,

workers, and employers have all held seats on ILO's Governing Body.

Delegates from the United States to the annual Conference are appointed by the President. Members of United States Delegations to other ILO meetings are usually appointed by the Department of State.

Under the amended ILO Constitution, additional responsibilities are placed on federal states, including the United States. Conventions and recommendations on questions falling within the jurisdiction of state and territorial governments rather than within the federal jurisdiction must now be submitted to the states and territories by the federal government.

International Telecommunication Union: ITU

Authorization. The United States participates in the reorganized ITU through ratification, deposited July 17, 1948, of the International Telecommunication Convention, signed at Atlantic City on October 2, 1947. This convention entered into force on January 1, 1949.

On May 31, 1947, the President designated the International Telecommunication Union as a public international organization entitled to enjoy the benefits of the International Organizations Immunities Act.

Payments. Contributions of the United States are paid from funds appropriated to the Department of State for this purpose. The contribution for 1953 was $142,000.

Agencies Chiefly Concerned. The Department of State is responsible for coordinating the interests of various other government agencies in connection with all matters pertaining to international telecommunications. This coordination is generally effected through the Telecommunications Coordinating Committee, which advises the Secretary of State and which consists of representatives of the following interested agencies: The Federal Communications Commission, the Department of the Treasury, Department of National Defense, Department of Commerce (Civil Aeronautics Administration), and the Department of State.

Participation. Since World War II, the United States has played an active role in bringing about a reorganization of the Union and in revising the radio regulations. It took the initiative in convening the Atlantic City Conferences for these purposes. Because of the provisions of Article 13 of the Atlantic City Convention stipulating that the telegraph regulations, telephone regulations, radio regulations, and additional radio regulations shall be binding on all members, the United States formally declared in the final protocol adopted by the Conference that it did not, by signature of the convention, accept any obligation in respect of the telegraph regulations, the telephone regulations, or the additional radio regulations.

United Nations Educational, Scientific and Cultural Organization: UNESCO

Authorization. A joint resolution, approved July 30, 1946, provided for membership and participation by the United States in UNESCO and authorized an appropriation therefor. In fulfillment of Article VII of the UNESCO Constitution, this resolution also authorized the establishment of a U.S. National Commission for UNESCO. On September 30, 1946, the UNESCO Constitution was signed for the United States and the instrument of acceptance was deposited with the British government. On May 31, 1947, the President designated UNESCO as a public international organization entitled to enjoy the benefits of the International Organizations Immunities Act.

Payments. The annual United States contribution is paid from funds appropriated to the Department of State for this purpose. The United States contribution for 1953 was $2,856,000.

Agencies Chiefly Concerned. The Department of State is the agency charged with primary responsibility in relation to UNESCO. The Library of Congress and the U.S. Office of Education also participate in the work of the organization.

Participation. Within the United States, the National Commission for UNESCO was established in September 1946, and is composed of members named by selected national organizations, officers of certain federal agencies, of state and local educational authorities, and members-at-large. It works with organizations and individuals in the development of UNESCO's work.

The UNESCO Relations Staff, provided by the Department of State, serves a dual function as the agency of liaison between UNESCO and the United States Government and as the secretariat for the United States National Commission.

International Bank for Reconstruction and Development: Bank

International Monetary Fund: Fund

Authorization. United States membership in both the Bank and the Fund was authorized by an act of Congress approved July 31, 1945. The United States signed the Articles of Agreement of the Bank on December 27, 1945, and of the Fund on December 20, 1945. This act also authorized the extension of certain immunities and privileges to the Bank and Fund and their members, authorized the payment of the subscription of the United States to the Bank, and set up, as the body to deal with Bank and Fund matters, a National Advisory Council on International Monetary Problems. Members of this Council are the Secretaries of Treasury (chairman), State, and Commerce; the chairman of the Board of Governors of the Federal Reserve System; the chairman of the Board of Directors of the Export-Import Bank of Washington; and the Administrator for Economic Cooperation.

On July 11, 1946, the President designated the Bank and Fund as public international organizations entitled to enjoy the benefits of the International Organizations Immunities Act.

Payments. The United States share in the subscribed capital of the Bank is $3,175,000,000 (20 per cent of which has been paid in), and its quota in the Fund is $2,750,000,000. There are no annual assessments for the Bank or Fund. The Bank meets expenses from income. The Fund meets expenses from earnings and capital.

Agencies Chiefly Concerned. Note *Authorization* above.

Participation. The United States has the right to appoint an Executive Director to the Bank in addition to the United States Governor. As a result of the subscription referred to above, this Director exercises 33.51 per cent of the voting power of all the directors.

The United States has the right to appoint an Executive Director to the Fund, in addition to the United States Governor. As a result of the quota referred to above, the United States Director at the present time exercises approximately 30 per cent of the total voting power of all Directors.

World Meteorological Organization:
WMO

Authorization. Following the consent of the Senate, the United States participation in WMO was authorized by certification of the WMO Convention on May 4, 1949.

Payments. The United States contribution to WMO is paid from funds appropriated to the Department of Commerce

(Weather Bureau) for this purpose. The United States contributed $36,253 to WMO in 1953.

Agencies Chiefly Concerned. The United States Weather Bureau of the Department of Commerce is the agency of the United States Government bearing chief responsibilities for our relations with and participation in WMO.

Participation. The United States Government is the depository for instruments of ratification to the WMO Convention. Members of the WMO Congress are represented by the heads of their meteorological services. In 1951 the first WMO Congress elected Dr. F.W. Reichelderfer, Chief of the United States Weather Bureau, its President.

Inter-Governmental Maritime Consultative Organization: IMCO
(*In preparatory stage as of July 1, 1953*)

Authorization. The United States instrument of ratification to the Convention on IMCO was transmitted to the Secretary-General of the United Nations on August 21, 1950. The Convention had been approved by the United States Senate on June 27, 1950. The IMCO Convention will come into force when twenty-one nations, of which seven shall have a total tonnage of not less than one million gross tons of shipping, have become parties to the Convention.

International Refugee Organization: IRO
(July 1, 1947 to January 31, 1952)

Authorization. A joint resolution of the Congress approved July 1, 1947, authorized United States participation in the IRO, which became effective July 3, 1947.

Payments. The United States paid its contributions from funds appropriated to the Department of State. Of the $398,596,802 contributed to IRO by member governments from February 1, 1947, to February 7, 1952, the United States contributed $237,116,355.

Participation. During the lifetime of IRO from July 1, 1947, to January 31, 1952, 1,045,750 persons left areas of operation for resettlement in new countries of residence. Of this number 343,419 were resettled in the United States.

Note: The United States Government continues to play a leading role in international refugee affairs. The United States is one of twenty members of the Intergovernmental Committee for European Migration, ICEM (originally Provisional Intergovernmental Committee for the Movement of Migrants from Europe), organized at Brussels in December 1951. The purpose of this organization is to facilitate the movement of surplus manpower from Europe to other countries where such manpower could be utilized. Congressional appropriations to the Mutual Security Act of 1951 included $10,000,000 to be used for moving surplus population from Western Europe. Five million of this was contributed to ICEM in 1952. The balance was to be contributed in 1953.

The United States participates in the United Nations Relief and Works Agency for Palestine Refugees (UNRWA), an organization established by the Fourth General Assembly of the United Nations on December 8, 1949. The UNRWA goal calls for a $250,000,000 relief and reintegration program from July 1, 1951, to June 30, 1954. The Mutual Security Act of 1951 approved the UNRWA program, and Congress appropriated $50,000,000 towards its accomplishment. $30,000,000 of this amount was paid in the fiscal year 1952. Payments on the remaining $20,000,000 were scheduled for 1953.

As a member of the United Nations, the United States shares in providing assistance of various kinds to refugees through The United Nations High Commissioner for Refugees.

International Bank bonds are brought to the attention of American investors.

APPENDIX

AIMS AND PURPOSES OF THE UNITED NATIONS

The aims and purposes of the United Nations are contained in the Preamble and Article I of the Charter, which read as follows:

WE THE PEOPLES OF THE UNITED NATIONS DETERMINED
to save succeeding generations from the scourge of war, which twice in our lifetime has brought untold sorrow to mankind, and to reaffirm faith in fundamental human rights, in the dignity and worth of the human person, in the equal rights of men and women and of nations large and small, and to establish conditions under which justice and respect for the obligations arising from treaties and other sources of international law can be maintained, and to promote social progress and better standards of life in larger freedom.

AND FOR THESE ENDS
to practice tolerance and live together in peace with one another as good neighbors, and to unite our strength to maintain international peace and security, and to ensure, by the acceptance of principles and the institution of methods, that armed force shall not be used, save in the common interest, and to employ international machinery for the promotion of the economic and social advancement of all peoples.

HAVE RESOLVED TO COMBINE OUR EFFORTS
TO ACCOMPLISH THESE AIMS,
Accordingly, our respective Governments, through representatives assembled in the city of San Francisco, who have exhibited their full powers found to be in good and due form, have agreed to the present Charter of the United Nations and do hereby establish an international organization to be known as the United Nations. . . .

The Purposes of the United Nations are:

1. To maintain international peace and security, and to that end: to take effective collective measures for the prevention and removal of threats to the peace, and for the suppression of acts of aggression or other breaches of the peace, and to bring about by peaceful means, and in conformity with the principles of justice and international law, adjustment or settlement of international disputes or situations which might lead to a breach of the peace;

2. To develop friendly relations among nations based on respect for the principle of equal rights and self-determination of peoples, and to take other appropriate measures to strengthen universal peace;

3. To achieve international cooperation in solving international problems of an economic, social, cultural, or humanitarian character, and in promoting and encouraging respect for human rights and for fundamental freedoms for all without distinction as to race, sex, language, or religion; and

4. To be a center for harmonizing the actions of nations in the attainment of these common ends.

Charter of the United Nations, Chapter IX

INTERNATIONAL ECONOMIC AND SOCIAL COOPERATION

Article 55

WITH A VIEW to the creation of conditions of stability and well-being which are necessary for peaceful and friendly relations among nations based on respect for the principle of equal rights and self-determination of peoples, the United Nations shall promote:

a. Higher standards of living, full employment, and conditions of economic and social progress and development;

b. Solutions of international economic, social, health, and related problems; and international cultural and educational cooperation; and

c. Universal respect for, and observance of, human rights and fundamental freedoms for all without distinction as to race, sex, language or religion.

Article 56

All members pledge themselves to take joint and separate action in cooperation with the organization for the achievement of the purposes set forth in Article 55.

Article 57

1. The various specialized agencies, established by intergovernmental agreement and having wide international responsibilities, as defined in their basic instruments, in economic, social, cultural, ed-

ucational, health, and related fields, shall be brought into relationship with the United Nations in accordance with the provisions of Article 63.

2. Such agencies thus brought into relationship with the United Nations are hereinafter referred to as specialized agencies.

Article 58

The organization shall make recommendations for the coordination of the policies and activities of the specialized agencies.

Article 59

The organization shall, where appropriate, initiate negotiations among the states concerned for the creation of any new specialized agencies required for the accomplishment of the purpose set forth in Article 55.

Article 60

Responsibility for the discharge of the functions of the organization set forth in this chapter shall be vested in the General Assembly and, under the authority of the General Assembly, in the Economic and Social Council, which shall have for this purpose the powers set forth in Chapter x.

Charter of the United Nations, Chapter x

THE ECONOMIC AND SOCIAL COUNCIL

COMPOSITION

Article 61

1. The Economic and Social Council shall consist of eighteen members of the United Nations elected by the General Assembly.

2. Subject to the provisions of paragraph 3, six members of the Economic and Social Council shall be elected each year for a term of three years. A retiring member shall be eligible for immediate re-election.

3. At the first election, eighteen members of the Economic and Social Council shall be chosen. The term of office of six members so chosen shall expire at the end of one year, and of six other members at the end of two years, in accordance with arrangements made by the General Assembly.

4. Each member of the Economic and Social Council shall have one representative.

FUNCTIONS AND POWERS

Article 62

1. The Economic and Social Council may make or initiate studies and reports with respect to international economic, social, cultural, educational, health, and related matters and may make recommendations with respect to any such matters to the General Assembly, to the Members of the United Nations, and to the specialized agencies concerned.

2. It may make recommendations for the purpose of promoting respect for, and observance of, human rights and fundamental freedoms for all.

3. It may prepare draft conventions for submission to the General Assembly, with respect to matters falling within its competence.

4. It may call, in accordance with the rules prescribed by the United Nations, international conferences on matters falling within its competence.

Article 63

1. The Economic and Social Council may enter into agreements with any of the agencies referred to in Article 57, defining the terms on which the agency concerned shall be brought into relationship with the United Nations. Such agreements shall be subject to approval by the General Assembly.

2. It may coordinate the activities of the specialized agencies through consultation with and recommendations to such agencies and through recommendations to the General Assembly and to the members of the United Nations.

Article 64

1. The Economic and Social Council may take appropriate steps to obtain regular reports from the specialized agencies. It may make arrangements with the members of the United Nations and with the specialized agencies to obtain reports on the steps taken to give effect to its own recommendations and to recommendation on matters falling within its competence made by the General Assembly.

2. It may communicate its observations on these reports to the General Assembly.

Article 65

The Economic and Social Council may furnish information to

the Security Council and shall assist the Security Council upon its request.

Article 66

1. The Economic and Social Council shall perform such functions as fall within its competence in connection with the carrying out of the recommendations of the General Assembly.

2. It may, with the approval of the General Assembly, perform services at the request of Members of the United Nations and at the request of specialized agencies.

3. It shall perform such other functions as are specified elsewhere in the present Charter or as may be assigned to it by the General Assembly.

VOTING

Article 67

1. Each member of the Economic and Social Council shall have one vote.

2. Decisions of the Economic and Social Council shall be made by a majority of the members present and voting.

PROCEDURE

Article 68

The Economic and Social Council shall set up commissions in economic and social fields and for the promotion of human rights, and such other commissions as may be required for the performance of its functions.

Article 69

The Economic and Social Council shall invite any Member of the United Nations to participate, without vote, in its deliberations on any matter of particular concern to that Member.

Article 70

The Economic and Social Council may make arrangements for representatives of the specialized agencies to participate, without vote, in its deliberations and in those of the commissions established by it, and for its representatives to participate in deliberations of the specialized agencies.

Article 71

The Economic and Social Council may make suitable arrangements for consultation with non-governmental organizations which are concerned with matters within its competence. Such arrangements may be made with international organizations and, where appropriate, with national organizations after consultation with the Member of the United Nations concerned.

Article 72

1. The Economic and Social Council shall adopt its own rules of procedure, including the method of selecting its President.

2. The Economic and Social Council shall meet as required in accordance with its rules, which shall include provision for the convening of meetings on request of a majority of its members.

Members of the United Nations and Their Membership in the Specialized Agencies

(June 1, 1954)

	ILO	FAO	UNESCO	WHO	BANK	FUND	ICAO	UPU	ITU	WMO	PC. IMCO
Afghanistan	x	x	x	x			x	x	x		
Argentina	x	x	x	x			x	x	x	x	x
Australia	x	x	x	x	x	x	x	x	x	x	x
Belgium	x	x	x	x	x	x	x	x	x	x	x
Bolivia	x	x	x	x	x	x	x	x			
Brazil	x	x	x	x	x	x	x	x	x	x	
Burma	x	x	x	x	x	x	x	x	x	x	
Byelorussia	x		x	x°				x	x	x	
Canada	x	x	x	x	x	x	x	x	x	x	x
Chile	x	x	x	x	x	x	x	x	x		
China	x		x	x°	x	x	x	x	x	x	
Colombia	x	x	x		x	x	x	x	x		
Costa Rica	x	x	x	x	x	x		x	x		
Cuba	x	x	x	x	x	x	x	x	x	x	
Czechoslovakia	x		x°	x°	x	x	x	x	x	x	
Denmark	x	x	x	x	x	x	x	x	x	x	
Dominican Republic	x	x	x	x	x	x	x	x	x	x	
Ecuador	x	x	x	x	x	x		x	x	x	
Egypt	x	x	x	x	x	x	x	x	x	x	
El Salvador	x	x	x	x	x	x	x	x	x		
Ethiopia	x	x		x	x	x	x	x	x	x	
France	x	x	x	x	x	x	x	x	x	x	x
Greece	x	x	x	x	x	x	x	x	x	x	x
Guatemala	x	x	x	x	x	x	x	x	x	x	
Haiti	x	x	x	x	x	x	x	x	x	x	
Honduras		x	x	x	x	x	x	x	x		
Iceland	x	x		x	x	x	x	x	x	x	
India	x	x	x	x	x	x	x	x	x	x	x
Indonesia	x	x	x	x			x	x	x	x	
Iran	x	x	x	x	x	x	x	x	x		

	ILO	FAO	UNESCO	WHO	BANK	FUND	ICAO	UPU	ITU	WMO	PC. IMCO
Iraq	x	x	x	x	x	x	x	x	x	x	
Israel	x	x	x	x			x	x	x	x	
Lebanon	x	x	x	x	x	x	x	x	x	x	
Liberia	x	x	x	x			x	x	x		
Luxembourg	x	x	x	x	x	x	x	x	x	x	
Mexico	x	x	x	x	x	x	x	x	x	x	
Netherlands	x	x	x	x	x	x	x	x	x	x	x
New Zealand	x	x	x	x			x	x	x	x	
Nicaragua		x	x	x	x	x	x	x	x		
Norway	x	x	x	x	x	x	x	x	x	x	x
Pakistan	x	x	x	x	x	x	x	x	x	x	
Panama	x	x	x	x	x	x		x	x		
Paraguay		x		x	x	x	x	x	x	x	
Peru	x	x	x	x	x	x	x	x	x	x	
Philippines	x	x	x*	x*	x	x	x	x	x	x	
Poland	x		x*	x*			x	x	x	x	
Saudi Arabia		x	x	x				x	x		
Sweden	x	x	x	x	x	x	x	x	x	x	x
Syria	x	x	x	x	x	x	x	x	x	x	
Thailand	x	x	x	x	x	x	x	x	x	x	
Turkey	x	x	x	x*	x	x	x	x	x	x	
Ukraine	x		x	x*				x	x	x	
South Africa	x	x	x	x*	x	x	x	x	x	x	
USSR	x		x	x*				x	x	x	
United Kingdom	x	x	x	x	x	x	x	x	x	x	x
USA	x	x	x	x	x	x	x	x	x	x	x
Uruguay	x	x	x	x	x	x		x	x	x	
Venezuela	x	x	x	x	x	x	x	x	x	x	
Yemen		x		x				x	x		
Yugoslavia	x	x	x	x	x	x		x	x	x	
60 members	55	54	56	59	48	48	50	60	60	47	12

* Have sent notification of withdrawal

Membership of United Nations Specialized Agencies

(June 1, 1954)

	UN* Member Countries	Non-Member* Countries	Territories	Total	Associate Members
ILO	55	14	....	69	
FAO	54	17.	---	71	
UNESCO	56	16	....	72	
WHO	59	22	---	81	3
BANK	48	7	---	55	
FUND	48	7	---	55	
ICAO	50	12	---	62	
UPU	60	22	11	93	
ITU	60	23	7	90	4
WMO	47	13	22	82	
PC. IMCO	12	---	---	12	

* Including countries which have withdrawn

Non-Members of the United Nations
and Their Membership in the Specialized Agencies

(June 1, 1954)

	ILO	FAO	UNESCO	WHO	BANK	FUND	ICAO	UPU	ITU	WMO
Albania				x°				x	x	
Algeria								x		
Austria	x	x	x	x	x	x	x	x	x	
Bulgaria	x			x°				x	x	x
Cambodia		x	x	x				x	x	
Ceylon	x	x	x	x	x	x	x	x	x	x
Finland	x	x		x	x	x	x	x	x	x
Germany (F.R.)	x	x	x	x	x	x			x	
Hungary	x		x°	x°				x	x	x
Indochina										x
Ireland	x	x		x			x	x	x	x
Italy	x	x	x	x	x	x	x	x	x	x
Japan	x	x	x	x	x	x	x	x	x	x
Jordan		x	x	x	x	x	x	x	x	
Korea		x	x	x			x	x	x	
Laos		x	x	x				x	x	
Libya	x	x	x	x			x	x	x	
Monaco		x		x					x	
Morocco				[x]						
Nepal		x	x	x						
Portugal	x	x		x			x	x	x	x
Rhodesia (S.)				[x]					x	
Roumania				x°				x	x	x
Spain		x	x	x			x	x	x	x
Switzerland	x	x	x	x			x	x	x	x
Tunisia				[x]				x		x
Vatican City								x	x	
Vietnam	x	x	x	x				x	x	
	14	17	16	22	7	7	12	22	23	13
			1°	4°						
			15	18						

° Have sent notification of withdrawal
[x] Associate member

Budgets of the Specialized Agencies
(Including Contributions by the United States)

Agency	1953 Budget	U.S. Share
International Labor Organization: ILO	$ 6,223,368	$ 1,538,991
Food and Agriculture Organization: FAO	5,250,000	1,673,750
United Nations Educational, Scientific and Cultural Organization: UNESCO	8,528,482	2,856,000
International Civil Aviation Organization: ICAO	2,817,167	815,112
International Bank for Reconstruction and Development: Bank	Meets expenses from income. (Administrative budget 1952-53 $5,712,000)	
International Monetary Fund: Fund	Meets expenses from earnings and capital. (Administrative budget 1952-53 $5,169,300)	
World Health Organization: WHO	8,485,095	2,866,667
Universal Postal Union: UPU	390,300	13,911
International Telecommunication Union: ITU	1,327,300	142,000
World Meteorological Organization: WMO	359,881	36,253

1954 Budget	U.S. Share	1955 Budget	U.S. Share

$6,311,170

$6,500,000

$9,461,449

$2,730,310

Meets expenses from income. (Administrative budget 1953-54 $6,079,000)

Meets expenses from earnings and capital. (Administrative Budget 1953-54 $5,140,500)

$8,497,700

$ 390,300 (1953)

$1,357,183

$ 360,000 (est.)

Additional Members of UPU, ITU, and WMO
(May 1, 1954)

In addition to the members listed on the foregoing charts, the total memberships of UPU, ITU and WMO include the following:

UPU

> Belgian Congo
> French Morocco
> French Overseas Territories
> Netherlands Antilles and Surinam
> Portuguese Colonies of West Africa
> Portuguese Colonies of East Africa, Asia and Oceania
> San Marino
> Spanish Morocco
> Spanish Colonies
> United Kingdom overseas colonies, protectorates and
>   territories under trusteeship
> United States possessions

---

11 members

ITU

> Belgian Congo and territory of Ruanda-Urundi
> French Protectorates of Morocco and Tunisia
> Overseas Territories of the French Republic and
>   territories administered as such
> Portuguese Overseas Territories
> Spanish Zone of Morocco and the totality of Spanish
>   possessions
> Colonies, Protectorates, Overseas Territories and
>   Territories under Mandate or Trusteeship of United
>   Kingdom
> Territories of United States
> (Netherlands, Surinam, Netherlands Antilles, New Guinea)

---

7 members

4 associate members: (1) Kenya, Uganda, Tanganyika
under United Kingdom trustee-
ship;
(2) Nigeria (including the Trust
Territory of the Cameroons

under United Kingdom Administration), Gold Coast (including the Trust Territory of Togoland under United Kingdom administration), Sierra Leone and
Gambia.

(3) Mayala—British Borneo Group
(4) Trust Territory of Somaliland
under Italian Administration

WMO

Belgian Congo
Bermuda
British Caribbean Territories
British Central African Territories (including Northern
Rhodesia, Nyasaland, Southern Rhodesia)
British East African Territories and Indian Ocean Islands
(including Kenya, Uganda, Tanganyika, Zanzibar,
Mauritius, Seychelles)
British Malaya—Borneo Territories (including Singapore,
Federation of Malaya, North Borneo, Sarawak,
Brunei)
British West African Territories (including Nigeria, Gold
Coast, Sierra Leone, Gambia)
French Cameroons
French Equatorial Africa
French Morocco
French Oceanic Colonies
French Somaliland
French Togoland
French West Africa
Hong Kong
Madagascar
Netherlands Antilles (Curacao)
New Caledonia
New Guinea (Netherlands Indies)
Portuguese East Africa
Portuguese West Africa
Surinam
(Argentina, including Malvinas)
(Australia, including Papua, Norfolk Island, New Guinea,
Nauru)

(Belgium, including Ruanda-Urundi)

(France, including Algeria, French Guiana, French West Indies, Reunion, Saint Pierre and Miquelon, Saar, Valleys of Andorra)

(Portugal, including Azores, Madeira, Cape Verde Is., Portuguese Guinea, S. Tome and Principe Is., Fortress of S. Joao Baptista de Ajuda, Portuguese India, Macao, Portuguese Timor)

(Spain, including Spanish West Africa and Valleys of Andorra)

(Union of South Africa, including Territory of South West Africa)

(United Kingdom of Great Britain and Northern Ireland, including Aden, Basutoland, Bechuanaland, British Solomon Is., Fiji, Gibraltar, Falkland Islands, Gilbert and Ellice Is., Malta, Swaziland)

---

22 members

SUGGESTIONS FOR FURTHER STUDY

It is hoped that the case studies presented herein have given the reader a better idea of the functioning of the Specialized Agencies at action level. It is the further hope that the reader will see fit to contribute to the understanding of world affairs by encouraging discussion groups, community organizations, and students to undertake similar studies. While it is essential that American citizens have some general knowledge of international institutions, it is not possible for each of us to be thoroughly skilled in all, desirable as that might be. But tracing the development of one problem confronting an international organization will give depth and perception to our judgments concerning all such institutions.

The Specialized Agencies appear to furnish the best framework within which to make such a study for the following reasons:

1. The activities in which the Specialized Agencies engage have their counterpart in our own neighborhood, no matter how isolated we may feel it to be. Our post office forwards our mail to the far corners of the world. Our telephone switchboard links us with millions of people outside our continental limits. We have our local problems of food supply, health services, working conditions, and transportation. Our banks engage in the financing of local enterprise much as the International Bank does across national boundaries. Tomorrow's weather is as important to us as it is to the captain of a large ocean-going vessel.

2. All of us have had actual contact with some of the local problems outlined above, so we can bring more or less expert opinion to bear on our study. This fact in itself quickens one's interest in the work of a particular Agency, whether he be a teen-ager dreaming of flying a jet, or a highly skilled pathologist searching for the origin of a baffling disease.

3. The history of the United States gives us a good perspective against which to weigh the work of the Specialized Agencies. In the exchange of peoples, ideas, goods, and services we have found it necessary to set up local, county, state, and national institutions to make these movements easier and more orderly. We have also learned that the workings of these institutions depend upon the mutual cooperation and good will of people, and that the institutions themselves should survive only if they serve the people. If we view the Specialized Agencies as international counterparts of those institutions that have been created within the nation, we can measure their successes and their failures against their services to the people of the world. Moreover, in moving toward the fulfillment of the American ideal we have combined the thoughts, talents, and energies of people representing every race, religion, and culture known to man. We have either solved, or are struggling with, the same problems that confront the Specialized Agencies as they seek the improvement of relationships among the neighborhoods of the world.

4. The *purposes, functions, activities,* and *influences* of international institutions should be stressed, as opposed to a *structural* survey of the organization. This latter approach is all too common among school and study groups. This does not mean that structure is to be ignored. In the action study approach, structure assumes its proper perspective as the vehicle of function. The purpose of the action study approach is not to produce apologists for everything done by international organizations, but to give the citizen a background in one organization that will better equip him to be constructively critical of all international institutions. The ideological and political conflicts that so frequently color and obscure the fundamental philosophies and purposes of international organizations are minimized in the Specialized Agencies, thus enhancing the opportunities for objective and impartial study.

5. Materials for the development of action studies are readily available. The suggestions that follow are starting points for the building of a resource library.

A. From the International Documents Service, Columbia University Press, 2960 Broadway, New York 27, New York (Official United Nations Sales Agent):

1. *How to Find Out About the United Nations,* 56 pp., (*15¢*). A valuable handbook that lists resources important to a study of the Specialized Agencies.

2. *Everyman's United Nations,* Third Edition, *1953,* ($1.50). A good basic reference text on the United Nations and Its Specialized Agencies.

3. *United Nations Bulletin,* published the first and fifteenth of every month at the United Nations. Subscription price $4.50 per year. Presents a concise current account of the Specialized Agencies and affords good background information on meetings and decisions.

4. *UNESCO Courier,* published monthly by UNESCO. Subscription price $2 per year. An excellent selection of feature articles and photographs, many of which deal with the work of the Specialized Agencies. The unusually high caliber of the photographs in the *Courier* make them particularly useful for bulletin boards and exhibits.

B. Letters should be directed to the Public Information Officer of each Specialized Agency explaining the fact that a resource file is being built and requesting catalogues of publications, free materials, sources of films and filmstrips that portray the work of the Agency, and addresses of national commissions or organizations directly concerned with the work of the Agency. Many of the Agencies have done excellent pamphlets concerning particular activities of the organization, some of which are available free of charge and in multiple copies where the purpose of their use is made known. Other Agencies have periodicals that will be sent free of charge to groups expressing interest in the work of the Agency. The Public Information Sections of these Agencies are very cooperative in answering specific questions regarding the Agencies. Address: The Public Information Officer at the following:

ILO, FAO, UNESCO, WHO, (UNICEF and IMCO) have offices at the United Nations, New York.

The International Headquarters of the Bank and Fund are located at 1818 H Street, N.W., Washington, D.C.

ICAO: International Aviation Building, Montreal, Canada.

UPU: Case Postale, Berne 14, Switzerland.

ITU: Palais Wilson, Geneva, Switzerland.

WMO: Campagne Rigot, Avenue de la Paix, Geneva, Switzerland.

c. To supplement these materials the resources of school and community libraries can be used for building a reference bibliography on conditions, activities, countries, and history of the action study decided upon. Articles appearing in newspapers and magazines should be clipped and filed for future reference.

d. As work progresses on the action study, it is possible to acquire helpful information and literature from the consular offices of the nations concerned as well as from private and public enterprises and organizations that may have an interest in the activity. Most governments have Information Divisions, and a letter addressed to the nation's capital city and directed to the Public Information Officer will establish correspondence.

e. In no other field is such excellent film and filmstrip work being done. To mention a few of the private concerns, associations, organizations, and governmental sources producing and distributing films on international affairs the author has used would be unfair to the dozens of others that could not be listed. Most libraries have standard reference books that review films and filmstrips as well as indicating the sources of supply. As a start, it is suggested that catalogues be requested from the following:

> Film and Visual Information Division
> Department of Public Information
> United Nations, New York

> Film and Visual Information Division
> U. N. E. S. C. O.
> 19 Avenue Kléber
> Paris 16, France

F. The American Association for the United Nations maintains a Public Correspondence Unit at the United Nations Headquarters in New York. The purpose of the Public Correspondence Unit is to service requests for information about the United Nations and its Specialized Agencies. Teachers, students, librarians, and study groups will discover this to be a most valuable resource. From time to time the Department of Public Information of the United Nations issues bulletins on the membership, budgets, and current activities of the Specialized Agencies. Copies of these bulletins may be requested of the Public Correspondence Unit. They will prove helpful in supplementing the data included as part of the Appendix to this book.

6. Action studies within the Specialized Agencies will take into account most of those understandings essential to a knowledge of world affairs. It has been the author's experience that such a study tends to lead toward the following goals:

a. A better understanding of global geography.

b. A better understanding of particular regions and areas in the world.

c. A better understanding of the world's supply of natural resources (including food) and their distribution.

d. A better understanding of other peoples, including their race, religion, culture, economic circumstances, and educational opportunities.

e. A better use of current events as reported by the press and other media.

f. An improvement in such basic skills as: map reading; use of globes and charts; use of radio, films, television, pamphlets and other media; acquiring information through research, correspondence, and personal interview.

7. One of the major difficulties encountered by those interested in education in the field of world affairs is that examples of international cooperation seem remote from the everyday life of the average citizen. On the other hand, the story of international conflict is reflected on every side: casualty reports, returning veterans, the draft, taxes, production figures, motion pictures, and headlines, to mention but a few. This paradox may best be illustrated by a high school student's remark: "Sure, it's all right to *talk* about this stuff, but what can we *do* about it?"

A well-developed action study in the Specialized Agencies lends itself to *action* in the following ways: A thorough study of this kind is a discipline which can have value for the individual as a new source of knowledge, pleasure, and interest; in gathering materials for community groups, schools, and libraries, one is creating resources that may be used by others for study; exhibits reflecting the work of the Agency may be arranged for the school and community; adults may find reasons for interesting themselves in the budgets of the Specialized Agencies by communicating their thoughts to their national legislators; young people may participate in the "Trick or Treat" program developed by UNICEF in which five hundred communities turned Hallowe'en energies into local-information and fund-raising campaigns for UNICEF (Details may be had by writing UNICEF, United Nations, New York); together, youth and adults may participate in any one of dozens of working field projects through the UNESCO Gift Coupon Plan (Details may be had from UNESCO, United Nations, New York); a study of this kind quickens one's sense of responsibility toward discussion groups, celebrations, and organizations that exist to further an understanding of world affairs.

Whatever approach one may take to a study of the Specialized Agencies, one is constantly aware of the fact that the Agencies afford an excellent example of how nations working together in applying *shared knowledge and techniques to solve mutual problems* are pointing the way toward world peace.

ACKNOWLEDGMENTS

The author wishes to express a particular indebtedness to the following people: Mrs. Bille-Brahe and Mr. and Mrs. Alfreds Rolavs for permission to use their names in chapter titles; Mr. Fred L. Rope, Public Affairs Officer, and Miss Mary Politzer, Assistant Public Information Officer, United States Mission to the United Nations; Miss Carol Moor, Librarian in Charge, United Nations Collection, New York University Law School Library, and her assistant Mr. Lu-Yu Kiang; Miss Marion Scott, Librarian, Westfield (N.J.) Senior High School; Mr. John Callahan, Dartmouth College '55; and to the personnel of the Department of Public Information, United Nations, whose resources and services made possible the photographs reproduced in the text other than those credited under the chapter acknowledgments below.

The illustrations on the jacket are reproductions of photographs of stamps issued by the United Nations Postal Administration. The UPU stamp was designed by H. Woyty-Wimmer of Thomas de la Rue & Co. of London and is manufactured by that firm. The REFUGEES and TECHNICAL ASSISTANCE stamps were designed by Olav Mathiesen, Staff Member Presentation Unit United Nations Secretariat, and are manufactured by Thomas de la Rue & Co. The FAO stamp was designed by Dirk Van Gelder and is manufactured by Thomas de la Rue & Co.

Generally speaking, the publications resources have been those of the United Nations and of the Agency concerned. The traditions of the International Civil Service restrict the identity of authors who prepare reports, journals, and releases for press and radio. It is the hope of the author that these people will recognize his appreciation of the excellence of their work as being reflected in the dedication. Where signed articles, or extensively used reports, have been drawn upon, notice of that fact has been included with appropriate chapter designations.

The author is indebted for much secretarial aid to Mrs. A. L. De-Schryver and Miss Mary Majcher.

The author's greatest obligations are to those two paragons of patience —one in the marts of trade, the other in the maze of marriage—Henry Schuman and Ellen Beckel.

People

During the making of this book, its author has had the benefit of the experiences of many people. The kindness of the following in replying to correspondence and their willingness to take time from busy schedules to explain the details of their work place him greatly in their debt: Miss Nora Jones and Dr. S. Y. Lin (FAO); Captain Robert N. Buck (Trans-World Airlines); Mr. S. G. Cooper (ICAO); Mr. Roberto Rendueles (WHO); Mr. Dickson Hartwell and Mrs. Dolores Vogeler (UNICEF); Mr. John H. Redding and Mr. John C. Allen (United States Post Office Department); Mr. Fulke Radice (International Bureau, UPU); Mr. Ed Allen and Mr. Snowden T. Herrick (ILO); Mr. Willy J. Dorchain (American Office, International Transport Workers' Federation); Mr. G. Marvin Wright and Mr. Walter H. Schwaikert (Long Lines Department, American Telephone and Telegraph Co.); Mr. Soemarno (Ministry of Information, Republic of Indonesia); Mr. Gerald C. Gross (ITU); Mrs. Jean Shaffner, Mr. Enrico Fulchignoni, Mr. D. J. Singh, Mr. Leo Fernig, Mr. Enrique Laguerre (UNESCO); Mr. James V. Fletcher (Bank); Mr. Jay Reid (Fund); Mr. T. R. Brooks and Mr. I. R. Tannehill (Weather Bureau, United States Department of Commerce); Cmdr. C.E.N. Franckom, D.B.E., R.N. (President, WMO Commission for Maritime Meteorology); Dr. G. Swoboda (Secretary-General, WMO); Mrs. Ruth S. Tropin (United States Office, Intergovernmental Committee for European Migrants); Senator H. Alexander Smith (New Jersey); Mr. Boris Ford (Technical Assistance Board, United Nations); Mr. Edmund H. Kellogg, Mr. G. Bernard Noble, Mr. E. Taylor Parks (Department of State); and Mr. C. L. Callander (National Advisory Council Secretariat).

Publications

CHAPTER 1

Food and Agriculture Organization. *FAO Fisheries Bulletin,* Vol. 5, No. 2, March-April 1952; *Activities of FAO Under the Expanded Technical*

Assistance Program, 1950-1952; *Constitution, Rules and Regulations,* February 1951

CHAPTER 2

International Civil Aviation Organization. *ICAO; Memorandum on ICAO,* Montreal, 1946; *Search and Rescue Manual,* Montreal, 1952

CHAPTER 3

World Health Organization. "A WHO/UNICEF Nurse in India," *WHO Newsletter,* January 1951

United Nations. *Final acts of the International Health Conference,* Lake Success, New York, October 1946

CHAPTER 4

A Brief History of the Development of the International Postal Service, United States Post Office Department, Washington, D.C., 1948

CHAPTER 5

O. Becu, ITF, *A Brief Survey of the History and Activities of the International Transportworkers' Federation,* International Transportworkers' Federation

International Labour Review; "The Special Tripartite Conference Concerning Rhine Boatmen," February 1950, pp. 105-117; "Second Session of the ILO Inland Transport Committee," June 1947, p. 560

International Labor Organization. *The International Labour Organisation, A Reference Handbook,* International Labour Office, Geneva, 1951

CHAPTER 6

Henry T. Killingsworth, "Overseas Telephone Service is 25 Years Old," *Bell Telephone Magazine,* Spring 1952

Federal Communications Commission. *Common Carrier Primer,* Washington, D.C., May 1951

CHAPTER 7

United Nations Educational, Scientific and Cultural Organization. *Conference Manual,* Paris, 1951; *Learn and Live,* Paris, 1951

CHAPTER 8

International Bank for Reconstruction and Development. *Articles of Agreement; Loans at Work,* Washington, D.C., July 15, 1950

CHAPTER 9

International Monetary Fund. *Articles of Agreement, International Monetary Fund,* Washington, D.C., 1952; *By-Laws and Rules and Regulations,* Eleventh Issue, Washington, D.C., 1951; *Schedule of Par Values,* Fifteenth Issue, Washington, D.C., 1952; *Annual Report,* 1952; *Summary Proceedings Annual Meeting,* 1952

CHAPTER 10

I. R. Tannehill, "The History and Status of the International Meteorological Organization (I.M.O.)," American Meteorological Society *Bulletin,* Vol. 28, No. 5, May 1947, pp. 207-219; "Meetings of the International Meteorological Organization (I.M.O.) in Toronto and Washington, 1947," Ibid. Vol. 29, No. 4, April, 1948, pp. 146-154
United States Department of Commerce (Weather Bureau). *Weather Forecasting,* Washington, D.C., February 1952
World Meteorological Organization. *WMO Bulletin,* Vol. 1, No. 1, April 1952

CHAPTER 11

International Refugee Organization. *Migration from Europe,* IRO General Council Document GC/199/Rev. 1, Geneva
United Nations Economic and Social Council. *Report of the International Refugee Organization,* E/2211, April 23, 1952, New York

CHAPTER 12

L. Delanney, "The United Nations Maritime Conference," *Transport and Communications Review,* Vol. 1, No. 1, July-September 1948
Department of State. *Toward a World Maritime Organization,* Publication 3196
United Nations. *United Nations Maritime Conference, Final acts and Related Documents,* Lake Success, New York, 1948
United States Senate, 80th. Congress, 2d Session. *Message from the President of the United States,* Executive 1, 1948

CHAPTER 13

United Nations, Department of Public Information. *United Nations Work and Programs for Technical Assistance,* United Nations, April, 1951

United Nations Economic and Social Council, *Expanded Programme of Technical Assistance*, Third Report of the Technical Assistance Board to the Technical Assistance Committee, E/2054, 19 July 1951; *Expanded Programme of Technical Assistance*, Fourth Report of the TAB to the Technical Assistance Committee, E/2213 (Vol. I), May 8, 1952

United Nations Technical Assistance Board. *The Expanded Programme of Technical Assistance for Economic Development of Under-Developed Countries*, United Nations, 1951

CHAPTER 14

Lincoln Palmer Bloomfield, "The Department of State and the United Nations," Department of State *Bulletin*, Vol. XXIII, No. 594, November 20, 1950

Department of State. *Participation of the United States Government in International Conferences* (July 1, 1947–June 30, 1948), Publication 3443, June 1949; *International Organizations in which the United States Participates* (1949) Publication 3655, February 1950

House of Representatives, 82d Congress, 2d Session. *Report of Activities of the National Advisory Council on International Monetary and Financial Problems*, House Document No. 523, United States Government Printing Office, Washington, 1952

Photographs

The Photographic and Visual Information Section, Department of Public Information, United Nations, supplied all photographs used in this book with the exception of the following:

CHAPTER 1

Photographs through courtesy of FAO.

CHAPTER 2

Photographs other than those of ICAO facilities through courtesy of Trans-World Airlines.

CHAPTER 4

Photographs of stamps courtesy of the United Nations Postal Administration.

CHAPTER 5

Photographs through courtesy of ILO.

CHAPTER 6

Photographs showing operations within the United States through the courtesy of the Long Lines Division of the American Telephone and Telegraph Company. Those showing operations abroad through the courtesy of the Ministry of Information, Republic of Indonesia.

CHAPTER 8

Photographs through the courtesy of the International Bank for Reconstruction and Development.

CHAPTER 9

Photograph of FUND Headquarters through the courtesy of that Agency.

CHAPTER 10

Photographs showing the personnel of the United States Weather Bureau are through the courtesy of that Bureau.

CHAPTER 14

Photograph of Postmaster General Montgomery Blair is through the courtesy of the United States Post Office Department.

INDEX